The Culture of Markets

Dedicated to the memory of my father, Mister Charlie

The Culture of Markets

Frederick F. Wherry

polity

First published in 2012 by Polity Press

Polity Press
65 Bridge Street
Cambridge CB2 1UR, UK

Polity Press
350 Main Street
Malden, MA 02148, USA

ISBN-13: 978-0-7456-4744-9 (hardback)
ISBN-13: 978-0-7456-4745-6 (paperback)

A catalogue record for this book is available from the British Library.

Typeset in 11 on 13 pt Sabon
by Servis Filmsetting Ltd, Stockport, Cheshire
Printed and bound in Great Britain by the MPG Books Group

The publisher has used its best endeavors to ensure that the URLs for external websites referred to in this book are correct and active at the time of going to press. However, the publisher has no responsibility for the websites and can make no guarantee that a site will remain live or that the content is or will remain appropriate.

Every effort has been made to trace all copyright holders, but if any have been inadvertently overlooked the publisher will be pleased to include any necessary credits in any subsequent reprint or edition.

For further information on Polity, visit our website: www.politybooks.com

Contents

Acknowledgments

While writing this book, I benefited greatly from my conversations with a number of scholars. Peggy Somers and I co-taught a graduate seminar at the University of Michigan on Cultural Approaches in Economic Sociology where we benefited from our interactions with one another and with the students in the Michigan Economic Sociology and Organizations Cluster. I also benefited greatly from my conversations with Viviana Zelizer, Alejandro Portes, Jeffrey Alexander, Nina Bandelj, Richard Swedberg, Fred Block, Dario Gaggio, and Lyn Spillman who shared their work with me while I was writing this book. Peggy Somers, Greta Krippner, Jason Owen-Smith, and Mark Mizruchi read some of the initial chapters from the book, and so too did James Furst who sent along links to *Newsweek*, *CNN Money*, and *The Wall Street Journal* to remind me how my work speaks to contemporary issues. James also reminded me to enjoy the writing process. Thank you, James.

I am indebted to Jonathan Skerrett at Polity Press who acted as an attentive and sensitive editor and to Susan Beer for her efficient and enthusiastic copy-editing. There are many others who should be thanked, so I must beg their forgiveness that their names do not appear here. Of course, any mistakes or shortcomings herein are my responsibility alone.

Acknowledgments

I owe much to my family for helping me stay balanced, especially my mom Peggy, my twin sister Frances, my brothers Bernard, Sam, Reggie, and Scott as well as my partner James, who has helped me see most things anew. This book is dedicated to the memory of my father, known to many as Mister Charlie, who passed away as this book project came to a close.

Introduction: Culture, Markets, and Economic Life

This book is about how culture shapes *markets*. But what does this look like in practice? One of the pitfalls that easily befall academic books is the emphasis on theory at the expense of demonstration – how are cultural theories about markets made manifest in real life? For this reason, we will turn to a comprehensive review of theories in the final chapter of the book and will only sketch some of the classical theories at this chapter's end. This will enable us to focus on empirical puzzles now and on how existing studies help us solve them, as the book proceeds.

In this chapter we begin with some illustrations of what culture looks like in the marketplace before moving to how culture makes a difference for "the bottom line" of profit. Then we move to brief discussions of market demand and supply from a cultural point of view. Next we turn to money and prices, re-casting these seemingly straightforward processes as anything but.

Let us begin with a description of Chrysler's turnaround in a recent *Newsweek* article. Stay attuned to the emphasis on the chief-executive-officer's charisma, the effect he has on his audience of employees who have gathered as if for a ritual ceremony. In this gathering, the CEO professes that he wants to create a "tribal" bond among the members of his top management.

[At Chrysler, the] workers now hang on [Sergio Marchionne's] words. Last month a sea of faces looked to their leader expectantly at company headquarters as 11,000 employees crowded to see him. Marchionne spoke about their status as survivors, recognizing aloud how hard he had pushed them. As he spoke of their commitment, his voice broke, forcing him to stop to regain control. After all, car guys don't cry ... [According to Marchionne, during that moment of silence,] 'not a chair moved, not a phone went off' as the crowd waited for him to continue ... [Marchione has] flattened the organizational structure [at Chrysler], creating a system – as he did first at Fiat – where 25 executives report directly to the chairman. It's his way, he says, of creating *a tribal bond* among top managers. (Berman, 2011)

In other words, the commitment to the product and the company goes beyond a rational calculation of how much one can benefit financially from being a part of Chrysler. A sense of obligation, a feeling of we-ness obtains among the managers, or at least this is one of the explicit goals of the company's head.

Even the macroeconomy seems to be wrapped up in meanings, public representations, costumes, postures, gestures, and tone. When the chairman of the Federal Reserve makes a speech, market watchers and market movers are attuned to the mood of his speech. The chairman's credibility comes not only from what he says and how well his statements are backed up by evidence but also from the manner in which he delivers his statement and how well he plays his part.

A word or phrase from the Fed chairman – or even *a gesture* – has the power to move financial markets ... *Every detail of his public presentation* will matter. Above all, he'll need to seem confident, even as he fields what's likely to be aggressive questioning, image consultants say. "It's unfortunate that you'd be judged on *posture, or looks, or tone,*" said Gerard Carney, head of U.S. financial communications for the PR firm Fleishman-Hillard ... As for his *attire*, it's best to stay simple and conservative at the press conference, said Michael Christian, an image consultant at Manhattan

Makeovers, who has written books under the name William Cane. Christian suggested a white shirt and a navy suit, which he said convey credibility. (Alden 2011)

It would seem that the market interface is a stage populated by sometimes colorful but sometimes dull characters. Some of these characters need a makeover in order to operate more effectively in the marketplace (Wherry, forthcoming). Markets are not merely technical accomplishments; they are cultural intentions that are inculcated, enacted, and that must (their audiences) engross.

Anthropologist Marshall Sahlins proposes that markets are cultural intentions. By this, he means that people within a society share loose understandings about how they should survive, how they should exchange, and what is appropriate for commercial exchange. He rejects the notion that markets are technical, efficient responses to a natural environment characterized by scarcity.

> [M]en do not merely "survive." They survive in a definite way. They reproduce themselves as certain kinds of men and women, social classes and groups, not as biological organisms or aggregates or organisms ("populations"). True that in so producing a cultural existence, society must remain within the limits of physical–natural necessity. But... not even the most biological of cultural ecologies can claim any more: "limits of viability" are the mode of practical intervention ... Within these limits, any group has the possibility of a great range of "rational" economic intentions, not even to mention the options of production strategy that can be conceived from the diversity of existing techniques, the example of neighboring societies, or the negation of either. (Sahlins 1976: 168)

From one society to the next, markets are organized differently, not because a physical–natural necessity or a lack of information about other societies precludes these markets from being structured otherwise.

It then should come as no surprise that economic sociologist Frank Dobbin finds a different *cultural intention* in the organization of the railways in the United States, Great Britain and France that cannot be explained post-hoc by the "limits of viability" of the physical-natural world in which the tracks are laid. As we shall see in Chapter 2, each country had access to the same technology and faced similar environmental constraints in their physical-natural worlds, yet in each country, the railway industry was organized differently, less centralized in the United States; more centralized in France and Great Britain.

There are a number of industries that could be organized in a centralized versus a decentralized. Take the example of healthcare. Debates have raged over whether the United States would benefit from a national healthcare system, whether a single-payer (centralized) system would work best in terms of efficiency, and why the United States' healthcare industry differs so dramatically from the healthcare industries in other Western industrialized countries with access to similar technologies and facing similar environmental (physical-natural world) constraints. This book shows why it is not merely a matter of politics and lobbying: there are deeply laid mental tracks orienting the direction that industries take when they are being organized or re-organized.

Industries follow different logics of operation, yet these logics and what is considered normative for a company, an industry, or an entire country are not necessarily consistent nor is there a broad consensus about how an industry should be organized. Roger Friedland and A. F. Robertson bring these insights together in *Beyond the Marketplace: Rethinking Economy and Society*, where they offer a telling example of how social norms are "transacted in daily life and are often bitterly contested" (Friedland and Robertson 1990: 37).

[There are] "different vocabularies of motive (loyalty, acquisitiveness, faith) and symbolic systems by which to create and measure

4

value (nation, money, religion) ... Every marketplace is assaulted, from time to time, by conflicting logics. Is the supply of oil, for example, to be regulated by profit-maximizing transnational corporations, by states seeking to conserve strategic resources, or according to the needs of people in households for heat, power, and transportation? In what sense is water a "public good" if the problem of scarcity is resolved by raising tariffs rather than by equitable rationing? (Friedland and Robertson 1990: 37)

A cultural understanding of market logics and of economic action more generally enables an investigation of markets that hones in what people actually do rather than what a narrow set of theories say they should. Meanings (cultural intentions) must be taken into account or those things we call markets cannot be reasonably understood.

Consider, too, the cultural intentions of consumers. In *The World of Goods* (1979), anthropologists Mary Douglas and Baron Isherwood remind us just how culturally infused the acts of buying and using goods can be. Through consumption, one glimpses "moral judgments about what a man is, what a woman is, how a man ought to treat his aged parents, how much of a start in life he ought to give his sons and daughters" (Douglas and Isherwood 1979: 37). On some occasions, one offers cash to another person; on other occasions, a gift, a drink, flowers. What a person exchanges has to be matched with the appropriate occasion; otherwise, the initiator of the exchange may become embarrassed or may find that her interlocutor refuses to consummate the transaction. These dynamics indicate that market exchange and consumption are thoroughly cultural affairs, and that everything cannot be reduced to a quantified dollar amount.

The failure to realize how culture constitutes the rules of consumption, pricing, and exchange has resulted in a number of baffling predicaments. For example, after Harley Davidson went from nearly going bankrupt to emerging as a highly demanded product in the 1980s, it seemed that the demand for Harleys resulted from the improved design of the engine and the marketing stories generated by branders. Other companies witlessly tried a similar strategy but failed to capture the imagination of consumers. Sociologist and marketing professor Douglas Holt explains that the demand for Harleys depends on its status as an icon, and that the product became an icon not only as a result of what the company did, but also as a consequence of what people active in their brand communities (recreational users of the product who establish voluntary associations of riders) did and how the myth of the rebel rider became authored by prominent films and television programs. This also happened to coincide with societal cultural disruptions – changes in how people saw themselves (see Chapter 1). It is this alchemy that explains the change in demand, and attempts to hunt down cool (as Malcolm Gladwell put it) cannot transform a product into an icon. Iconic products have their congregants of believers who are using the product to deal with the times in which they live. Technical fixes and savvy marketing messages are not enough to influence demand. Companies that ignored the rituals and the various groups that generated their product's brand value did so at their peril.

We find similar missteps as the US government tries to satisfy its electorate with tax cuts. A survey on people's perceptions of the Administration's tax policies revealed that much of the voting public was unaware that they had received a tax cut. How could this be? The numbers don't lie. A person either pays more or less than she previously did in taxes. It turns out that the way that people account for their money has less to do with total dollar amounts and more to do with *how* the tax cut was administered and what it was called. Had they received a single check (a windfall gain), the average consumer would have felt the satisfaction of the cut; however, by receiving modest reductions each month in their payroll tax obligations, they did not feel that they had been given anything. It does not matter that the total amount they received over the course of twelve months in small deductions might have exceeded what they would have received in a one-time payment.

These mental accounting heuristics bring to light the cultural meanings of money. How people understand money, prices, savings, investments, and debt have less to do with the mathematics of what is in the bank account or the expected value of a loss versus a gain. And people use money to do more than just purchase goods and services. Sometimes money becomes the basis for sociability, a way to mark membership in a community, or a way to confer appreciation. It should, therefore, come as no surprise that American Express has its own social currency, other credit cards offer loyalty points, airlines offer frequent flier miles, and some communities issue their own community dollars. The marketplace and the currencies that facilitate exchange are multi-vocal sites for the affirmation, generation, and transformation of meanings.

What Culture Is

Paul DiMaggio offers a useful definition of culture: "social cognition, the content and categories of conscious thought and the taken-for granted" (DiMaggio 1990: 113). Let's take a look at each component of this broad definition. By social cognition, DiMaggio means that what people believe and the attitudes they hold, along with they way that they evaluate behaviors and things, are socially constituted. Just as people are born into a culture with a language and a structure of language that existed before they were born, so too do individuals find themselves by birth or by migration to inhabit a shared sense about how the world is ordered (or at least about how things ought to be ordered and done).

Much of the way that people experience the world is through the categories we have about what goes together and what should remain separate. These categories have boundaries and people often take them for granted. For example, there is a categorical boundary between people and things. We can imagine that most things should be sold, unless we are talking about the Declaration of Independence. It is now generally understood that people should not be auctioned off as if they are cattle, and when slavery existed, it was made possible by re-defining the category of human person so that there were some biological humans who were not considered to be culturally as full human beings. These modes of categorization make bidding for organs for those needing organ transplants or auctioning off babies in the adoption market to be nearly unthinkable. There are ways that this can be accomplished technically and there may even be arguments for how safeguards could be put into place so that the adoption market only allowed safe bidders to participate, but the categorical boundaries render these exchanges null.

Finally, there are ways of seeing the world and one's place in it that preoccupies cultural approaches to markets. Paul DiMaggio uses an essay written by Thurmond Arnold in the late 1930s to illustrate that how people approach work and organizations depends on their interpretive frames. Arnold writes:

> The transition from the life of a trial lawyer to that of a professor at the Yale School of Law [was] a most interesting one. The academic life was different from practice in that the scholarly heroes were men who dug up little sections of truth for the love of it – a purely monastic ideal. Yet this mythology was tempered and molded by the great overshadowing divinity, the American Businessman. Yale was doing what it could to search for truth in the same organized efficient way in which the United States Steel Corporation made steel. There was much about Yale in 1930 in common with the Rotary Club of Laramie, Wyoming, from which the writer hailed. "Service" was the watchword and the organized "project" was the crusade. (quoted in DiMaggio 1990: 120)

The marketplace is not simply a place where money is made; it is a site of service, a place where crusades and social movements attempt to overturn "bad" practices. From one institution to the next, there is a creed, a set of principles about how one should behave and what the various modes of behavior mean.

What Markets Are

In this book, we use the term market loosely. Sometimes, markets are specific sites where goods are bought and sold. At other times, markets are abstract spaces where people assume the roles of buyer or seller, third party monitors or regulatory enforcers. One can imagine a flea market, an auction, a handicraft market, outdoor markets, or even malls and large superstores as sites where things are placed on sale and buyers come to purchase them. These sites vary in whether the prices are fixed or negotiated, and even the style of talking about prices and value varies from one type of market to the next. Sometimes prices are prominently displayed; at other times, prices are nowhere to be found as a face-to-face negotiation establishes what it will be. Sometimes prices are held up as more important than quality, and at other times, prices seem too vulgar to attach to the goods or services on offer.

Markets are also virtual, found online, with symbols, photographs, personalities, and staged events that give these markets a sense of character, and that allows participation in these markets to become a form of play. E-Bay has a different character and interface than Craigslist, and these markets vary rather significantly from the exchange of stocks and futures on TD Ameritrade.

Karl Polanyi informs how we think about markets. Markets have varied over time in the logics that organize them. The logics of exchange and self-regulation characterize the modern capitalist markets of today, but other central principles have organized markets in various places at different periods of time.

> This cursory outline of the economic system and markets, taken separately, shows that never before our own time were markets more than accessories of economic life . . . The self-regulating market was unknown; indeed the emergence of the idea of self-regulation was a complete reversal of the trend of development. It is in light of these drafts that the extraordinary assumptions underlying a market economy can alone be fully comprehended. (Polanyi [1944] 2001: 71)

Polanyi argues that markets are a cultural phenomenon because the *belief* in a market that self-regulates did not magically emerge among market participants. It was consciously worked on, so that whenever the market mechanism seemed that it would collapse because capitalist owners of companies had gone too far in exploiting the workers in their factories, the national government would step in to assuage the sufferings of workers and to offer explanations for why the market works the way it does and how the self-regulating markets could benefit all involved.

What the Classics Say

It is helpful to take a moment to think about what Emile Durkheim, Max Weber, and Karl Marx have had to say about culture and markets. While the concluding chapter will go into more depth regarding sociological theories that inform the case studies in this book, this section will sketch how these thinkers have shaped the types of questions we now ask about culture and markets.

In the first edition of the *Handbook of Economic Sociology* (1994), Neil Smelser and Richard Swedberg identify Durkheim's understandings of the economy as "less comprehensive and systematic" (11) than that of Max Weber. Durkheim's most important contribution to economic sociology, in their reading, is *The Division of Labor in Society* ([1893] 1984) because it rejects the notion that the division of labor serves only the economic function of generating wealth and optimizing efficiency. For Durkheim, social solidarity and cohesion result from the division of labor. As the division of labor increases, the interdependencies of one unit with its others also increases, and this generates the need for rights and duties that ensure cooperation.

Smelser and Swedberg also acknowledge that "rituals, feasts, and other solidarity-enhancing mechanisms" and an economy based on morals are essential for society's cohesion, but they do not go into detail as to what Durkheim means by morality or how ritual and religion work in modern economies. Durkheim wrote that in pre-modern times, people understood what we now call private property as something that belongs to the gods (Durkheim [1957] 2005: 121–220). These religious beliefs transformed land and later private property into sacred objects needing protection from defilement. Between his ideas found in *Professional Ethics and Civic Morals* ([1957] 2005) and those found in *The Elementary Forms of Religious Life* ([1912] 1995), Durkheim had established that consumption and the constitution of an object as somehow worthy of collective protection derived its logic from ritual and non-market beliefs. In modern times, this linkage has been stretched into a fanatical protection of property rights and a missionary-like zeal for proselytizing free market principles. Among economic sociologists, Viviana Zelizer arguably goes furthest in showing how sacred and profane distinctions are made about life insurance and how currencies are created to hold not only economic value but also religious, magical, and social beliefs.

The chapters in this book take on Durkheim's work as some of the case studies dwell on shared understandings within

11

industries or across entire societies that shape how companies organize production. Just as Durkheim acknowledged a shift from organic to mechanical solidarity, some of the case studies in this book note a movement from normative to rational logics in the discourse of large companies in the United States. And just as Durkheim focused on rituals and the generation of solidarity, this book shows how consumers participate in rituals, form brand communities, and generate a shared consciousness of kind as they buy, talk about, and ritually celebrate meaningful objects.

From Max Weber we have both an analysis of meaningful action in the marketplace and of the role that religious values, in this case, those of ascetic Protestantism, play. One's vocation was a calling, performed as if done unto God. And financial stewardship was a way of accepting God's gifts respectfully. Monies earned should not be spent on "lazy restfulness" or "sinful enjoyment" (Weber [1905] 2008: 146), and as one acquires wealth, one illustrates how God blesses the chosen ones and those called to His purpose. This is the spirit of market participation that facilitated the rise of capitalism.

The attempt to capture the spiritual teachings guiding market behavior have since been captured by a number of scholars, including Francis Sutton and his collaborators in *The American Business Creed* (1956). They review materials from 1948 and 1949 that illustrate how American businesspeople are not simply motivated by profit as they present a favorable image of their virtues, but that they are also trying to resolve a sense of conflict between their own religious beliefs and the imperative to ignore the betterment of others for self-gain. These moral strains and the attempts of people to resolve them have opened the way for such probing analyses as that of Robert Wuthnow's *Poor Richard's Principles* (1996) on how business people imbue their work with moral meanings and forthcoming work by Lyn Spillman on how business associations promote solidarity and generate collective understandings. This strand of research takes religious and other beliefs seriously as motivating people to work and as providing justifications for why their behaviors might look to an outsider to be in conflict with their moral values, but their behaviors may nonetheless be morally understandable within the context of the ethos in which they operate as an insider to a company and its imperatives.

In a well-known passage from *Economy and Society* ([1922] 1978), Max Weber outlines the social orientation of economic action. Analogously, consumer demand is social in that the consumer implicitly takes account of others. The social orientation of action takes four forms: (1) through instrumental maneuvers with (or against) someone else to realize a goal (*Zweckrational*); (2) the social conventions and ingrained habits making the consideration of some goods or services unthinkable (convention; ingrained habituation); (3) the emotions stirred through interaction enhancing or diminishing the attractiveness of a good or service (affection); or (4) collectively held transcendental beliefs rendering some things nearly invaluable or certainly priceless (*Zwertrational*). These four pathways remind us as sociologists to interpret the meanings that actions have for the people concerned, and it is in this realm of meaning that we find the culture of markets and of market action.

Finally, Karl Marx offers a materialist reading of the culture of markets. By this, I mean that he focuses on who owns the means of production and how these owners manipulate the labor resources of workers and the beliefs that workers have in order to maximize the profits that these captains of capital can capture. Sahlins (1976: 168–9) interprets Marx's *German Ideology* ([1835] 2004) to mean that Marx himself understands the limits of historical materialism. The physical world's limits have both an objective and a subject character. In the subjective character one finds cultural meanings and social relationships. The objective and the subjective must be considered simultaneously in order to understand the "mode of production" as "a definite form of activity of [...] individuals, a definite form of expressing their life, a definite *mode of life* on their part" (Marx and Engels [1835] 2004: 42).

Marxists orientations toward markets have led to studies of culture as facilitating the supply of cheap labor and of branding as simply another instance in which people are exploited. In the first, we have such authors as C. K. Lee writing about factory workers in China and Hong Kong. Factory managers use local cultural understandings about family and gender to manufacture consent among the workers, reducing the wages of labor itself as well as the costs associated with monitoring and disciplining workers. Such authors as George Ritzer and Juliet Schor have honed in on the manipulation of cultural images and understandings to sell products and to cloak the devastations of market capitalism.

The Organization of the Chapters

The meaningful world of markets requires that we re-think what market demand means and the motivations and possibilities for market suppliers. In the first chapter, we ask why people want the things they do. After demonstrating the historically contingent, the ritual-like purposes, the relationship-building, and the manipulative aspects of consumption, we will move to Chapter 2 to examine the dynamics of supply. Why do companies organize themselves in the ways that they do to produce goods and services? What are the meanings and the mechanisms that enable the suppliers of goods to function in different types of markets? Chapter 3 turns to the meanings imbued in money and prices, showing that money is more than a way to obtain goods and services and that people account for their money using more than mathematical logics. Then Chapter 4 details how one conducts cultural analyses of markets. What should the analyst look for and what are the data that a cultural analyst examines? The concluding chapter offers a sweeping overview of key concepts explored in this book and pushes us toward a cultural sociology of markets. Upon completing *The Culture of Markets*, one should be able to look at economic problems with fresh eyes and perhaps rediscover markets as the meaningful spaces of exchange that they are. Now let us turn to the challenge of pushing the cultural dimensions of markets to the fore, where their contours and dynamics can be more clearly perceived.

1

The Cultural Roots of Market Demand

Why do groups of people want similar things? Shared meanings, social contexts, and common strategies of action influence what people do, including what they buy. A style of dress becomes wildly popular then utterly passé. To be popular is to be adopted by groups of people; and to have market appeal (even if it is a small market of buyers operating in their own niche of taste) is to have an audience that feels it has meaningful ties to a good or service. This chapter elaborates three ways that market demand is generated and maintained.

(1) People come to understand what they want through their interactions with others (*social networks*) and through their commitment to the values of their *brand communities*. Social networks form among people sharing common stories and understandings about why they are tied together; and consumption behaviors get distributed through these social networks like a virus with the taste for fatty foods, for instance, spreading obesity among friends and family; moreover, people interact with one another in ritual-like ways generating a sense of community around objects, including commercial goods. For people in brand communities, shared stories, symbols, and meaningful gatherings reinforce their commitment and desire to protect the integrity of their treasured brand.

(2) *Accidents of history* generate consumer demand; for example, government policies make goods easier (or harder) to obtain; political struggles over acknowledgment and over the direction a company takes affect the availability of a product or service; and ingrained habits make switching to other (technically better) products more difficult. These acts generate collective myths about why a good is popular with a particular population, such as beer for the British but wine for the French; the hearty American breakfast versus light Continental fare. Historical accidents get locked into the consumption habits of subpopulations and entire societies.

(3) Marketers and business owners *manipulate consumers* into buying goods by focusing on the meanings, images, and symbols that make a product or service appealing for different demographic groups. Marketers take culture seriously and conduct on-the-ground research to identify how consumers use goods creatively to mark their identities and to differentiate themselves from members of other groups; moreover, department stores are designed to take into account how people see the world, what meanings they imbue in spatial layout, and how people place themselves in selling spaces so that their shopping experiences help them to become their imagined selves.

After reviewing these three pathways to generating and maintaining demand, the chapter will examine how people account for their purchase decisions. What people are willing to pay for what they want follows cultural and social logics that defy common sense: a dollar is not simply a dollar that can be used in any way that an individual pleases. Thinking about what ought to be done and how the money became available in the first place constrain individual calculations about what constitutes "a good buy." To these insights we now turn.

Social Ties, Brand Communities, and Market Demand

This section begins with a description of networks that allow consumer demands to spread through contagion. This depiction of tastes as moving like viruses through intimate contact does not privilege the culture of these network configurations; therefore, these depictions of networks as conduits of taste will be followed by explicit examples of how culture cements these social ties and orients people to want different things in circuits of exchange, in ritual like interactions, and in brand communities.

Paul DiMaggio and Hugh Louch (1998) have demonstrated the importance of social ties for consumers who look to people they know to search for goods and services. Although they bracket why people demand the goods and services that they do, the authors offer evidence that people generally talk to people they know about the purchases they should make. Informal social ties function as a form of insurance against the risks buyers incur in an otherwise seemingly anonymous marketplace. Informal social ties rank along side of brand names and warranties as devices on which consumers rely to protect themselves while making transactions, for they minimize the cost of information and thereby reduce the likelihood of malfeasance on the part of the seller.

DiMaggio and Louch suggest not only that "birds of a feather flock together" but also that if one bird coughs, her network neighbors will catch a cold. Other social scientists have gone further in demonstrating the viral nature of consumer preferences within the network structure. Along these lines of research, Nicholas Christakis and James Fowler (2007) studied over 12,000 people and their networks from 1971 to 2003 and found that when one's spouse, sibling, or friend became obese, the linked individual also became at risk for obesity. These findings suggest that the revealed preference for fatty foods versus exercise spreads through network ties like any other epidemic might. In a similar size study (2008), the authors found that the decision to quit smoking is a collective one that affects others within the network by virtue of being tied directly or indirectly to individuals expressing a changed consumption preference.

Eating fatty foods at fast-food restaurants and smoking cigarettes are behaviors that spread through network ties, but the emergence of these activities as appropriate for particular networks is not random. French sociologist Pierre Bourdieu (1984) has shown that the tastes that people have for different types of art, movies, houses, and food depend on both their economic and cultural capital. When people are asked to rank images that they found beautiful or to comment on less versus more abstract forms of art, they tend to converge in their taste according to their accumulations of economic and cultural capital. In other words, people with lots of education (embodied cultural capital) have different tastes from those of people with less; and in these two groups, there is another split between people with higher and lower wealth/income (economic capital). On the one hand, one needs to have money (economic capital) in order to afford some luxury goods and to be able to travel to exclusive vacation destinations. On the other hand, one needs to know how to behave when consuming the luxury good or when staying for the weekend in a fifteenth-century palace in Venice. A person may be able to afford a house in the south of France with a wine cellar, but will that same person know how to talk about and entertain with the wine cellar in a way that her socially significant others deem appropriate? If the American restaurant's menu is written only in French, will the patron show a sense of ease in ordering from it?

It is often in the existing social network that an individual learns how to use goods properly and why those goods are so enjoyable. Take the example of marijuana smoking. According to Howard Becker (1953), marijuana smokers use their social ties with other smokers to learn *why* smoking is enjoyable, in part, because the pleasure is neither always obvious nor always physically based. From one's coevals one learns what the physical indications of pleasure might be and because socially relevant others are seen enjoying themselves, a first time user of marijuana is more likely to try the substance in the future even if she does not enjoy her first or second experience with the substance. Because marijuana is not physically addictive like cigarettes are, it offers a strong case in favor of social (versus physical) bases of taste.

Building on the work of Pierre Bourdieu, sociologist Omar Lizardo (2006) examines how acquired tastes and niche tastes are generated through network ties but depend on shared understandings among members of the network. Acquired and niche tastes correspond to strong social ties; dominated tastes, a combination of strong and weak ties. Acquired tastes require cultivation and the help of knowledgeable insiders so that those acquiring the taste can learn how to enjoy what might otherwise be un-pleasurable. Similarly, niche tastes require great investments of time to become familiar with *symbols* and *usage customs* not widely understood outside of the niche.

These investments of time and the acquisition of specialized knowledge mean that these goods and services have high levels of asset specificity. Asset specificity refers to particularities Oliver E. Williamson (1981: 555) is a transactions costs economist who writes about asset specificity, and he explains it this way: "The issue is less whether there are large fixed investments [...] than whether such investments are specialized to a particular transaction. Items that are unspecialized among users pose few hazards, since buyers in these circumstances can easily turn to alternative sources and suppliers can sell output intended for one buyer to other buyers without difficulty." Lizardo translates these insights about asset specificity to mean that highbrow cultural tastes should correspond with high asset specificities (specialized understandings about usage norms, symbols, and shared stories) and be susceptible to a person's strong social ties. By contrast, popular tastes correspond with low asset specificities and are therefore subject to a person's weak (arm's-length) social ties. Presumably, knowledge about how to use a good or service properly and what the narratives are about why its use is worthwhile are so widespread that special investments of time and energy are not needed.

Paul DiMaggio (1990) notes that Thorstein Veblen understands tastes as a function of status competition with individuals looking up to see what those with more prestige consume but also looking down to avoid consuming what those with less status enjoy. This "vertical interdependence" of tastes, however, does not take social structure into account: "[P]eople embedded in durable and close-knit social networks need fewer status cues than those whose interactions are characteristically more fleeting, and therefore are likely to invest less in status commodities or cultural capital" (DiMaggio 1990: 126). This leads DiMaggio to consider the dynamics of people within the same status group looking at one another to gather cues about what to consume (horizontal interdependence).

A qualitatively different way of looking at tastes and social ties is through the concept of circuits. Viviana Zelizer developed the concept of the circuit in order to understand how people interact with one another, using different forms of currency and different consumption goods to mark themselves as being in particular types of relationships or in a particular type of community. A circuit differs from a network in that the latter is a set of sites connected to one another through one- or two-way exchanges, while the latter is a set of dynamic, meaningful, and constantly negotiated relations. Circuits require qualitative investigation into meanings whereas networks can be investigated quantitatively. By qualitative investigation, I am referring to the nicknames that people in circuits give the things they exchange, the categories of relationships they believe themselves to be in, and the negotiations they have around what types of money, goods, and services are appropriate for exchange among what categories of persons within the circuit.

In bounded family circuits, for example, how the demand for different types of goods emerges manifests itself as a means to maintain and honor interpersonal relations. Zelizer shows, for example, why an individual may decide to purchase a "fancy coffee maker" capable of compressing espresso ground beans and steaming whole milk foam although a regular coffee maker has satisfied the individual's needs thus far. She draws on Christopher Carrington's interviews with gay and lesbian households in the San Francisco Bay Area to demonstrate how purchases become justified as a way to make a loved one feel cared for. In the example, Federico Monterosa had resisted buying a fancy coffee maker because the cheap one they owned worked fine, but Federico's domestic partner convinced "Freddy" to do so as a way of working on his relationship with his parents, especially his mom.

> Freddy's parents were coming to San Francisco and were planning to stay with us. Freddy's mom likes coffee, and so I made the case that we should buy a nice coffee maker to make her feel at home... because it was kind of hard on her when Freddy came out to her and all. With that, he agreed and we went to Macy's and bought a decent coffee maker. (Carrington 1999 in Zelizer 2005: 236)

The individual has oriented his action not only toward his own needs or tastes but also toward the different social relations that will be built, maintained, or honored through the particular purchase. In this way, his demand for the fancy coffee maker is socially situated and would not be intelligible outside of the relationships he holds dear, the informal sanctions that his family might impose on him for not making his mother feel at home (disapproving remarks, the "cold shoulder," the "cold bed," etc.), and what he thinks the coffee maker will symbolize for his mother.

On the dating circuit, we see even more qualitative distinctions being made among different categories of relationship. The seriousness of the relationship corresponds with the types of gifts the lovers exchange. Their demand for these gifts depends not only on their idiosyncrasies but also on what one "ought" to give a person categorized as a fiancé versus an individual who functions as a friend-with-benefits (a sexual relationship with friendship but without the expectation of a long-term or exclusive commitment). If a man, for example, gives a ring to a friend-with-benefits, he might discover that the friend is shocked and that his friends and family are outraged. One does not make that type of purchase for this type of thing: the relationship category does not match the canon of goods purchased and exchanged. In this way, markets are moral because consumers have a sense of some matches being right but others wrong for people like themselves (Fourcade and Healy 2007).

Even the demand for commercial sex work relies more on how that work is categorized than on the physical attributes of the worker and the corresponding prices for services rendered. In *The Purchase of Intimacy* a commercial sex worker describes how her clients responded negatively to the offer of a discount and a "free ride."

> They pretend to be flattered, but they never come back … There was one client I had who was so sexy, a tai-chi practitioner, and really fun to fuck. Since good sex is a rare thing, I told him I'd see him for $20 (my normal rate is $250). Another guy, he was so sexy, I told him "come for free." Both of them freaked out and never returned. (Zelizer 2005: 128)

In the world of supply and demand, one would think that if the services one enjoyed previously from the same supplier had suddenly fallen in price, one would enjoy more of the service. The category of commercial sex work, however, offers such an impermeable boundary within the context of a socially legitimate relationship, that such reductions in price disrupt demand by mismatching the category of relations with a different bundle of exchange media; in other words, commercial sex work for the customer in question involves the exchange of money (legal tender) for sex; it does not involve the exchange of discounts, gifts, pendants, rings, or other exchange media. Her mismatch of the exchange media with the category of relationship dissolves his demand for her services.

While Viviana Zelizer focuses on circuits, sociologist Randall Collins hones in on interaction rituals and how they build up, generating an emotional attachment between individuals engaged in the rituals and the objects used in the ritual process. Collins does not use the term ritual to describe a religious event, but instead notes that there are many interactions that people have that seem to follow a script and that veering away from the script often has consequences as the believers and participants in the ritual sanction the wrongdoer.

Interaction Ritual Chains (IRCs) are an observable process in which individuals generate emotional energy, group symbols, and symbolic boundaries (see Goffman 1967). Collins (2004: xiii) implies that differences in emotional energy from one buying situation to the next make the buyer perceive a good or service as more attractive than its potential substitute. Emotional energy itself is "a strong steady emotion [sentiment, or affect], lasting over a period of time ... [that] gives the ability to act with initiative and resolve, to set the direction of social situations rather than to be dominated by others in the micro-details of interaction ... [and] to be self-directed when alone" (Collins 2004: 134). These differences in emotional energy lead to such distinctions as the sacred and the profane as well as the boundaries between in- and out-groups.

The Interaction Ritual Chains perspective embeds the demand for goods and services in the social situations where those goods and services are consumed. To the extent that these consumption contexts take on a character of their own, the consumer engages in a dynamic circuit of commerce. Some cigar smokers, for example, wear smoking jackets, retire to their smoking room, and relax with other smokers at an informally designated time of day. These leisure rituals generated the emotional energy that helped sustain the desire for smoking beyond any physiological craving for tobacco. Therefore, to understand the demand for goods and services one has to take into account the patterned interactions where consumers use, discuss, or eye these goods and services.

The ritual-like behaviors that generate and maintain demand for particular goods and services have been theorized as responsible for the formation of brand communities. Albert Muniz and Thomas O'Guinn are marketing and advertising professors trained in sociology. They define brand communities as "specialized, non-geographically bound [groups], based on a structured set of social relationships among admirers of a brand ... Like other communities, it is marked by a shared consciousness, rituals, and traditions, and a sense of moral responsibility" (Albert M. Muniz and O'Guinn 2001: 412).

One of the ways that they demonstrate the consciousness of kind among members of a brand community is through their interviews with Mac computer users. A forty-year-old academic defined herself as an outsider, unlike the "IBM people" who wore boring suits and voted Republican. She and others felt that their use of a Mac pushed against a dominant Microsoft, like a David fighting Goliath, and they employed a language of purity and pollution when describing the differences between a Mac and a PC: the former is pure, free from viruses; the latter is impure, susceptible to hacker violations, viruses, and crashes.

Muniz and O'Guinn find that loosely scripted rituals "perpetuate [a] consciousness of kind" (422) among the users of a brand. Saab drivers engaged in greeting rituals when they encountered other Saab drivers, for example:

GEORGE If you drove a Saab, whenever you passed someone else driving a Saab on the road, you beeped or flashed your lights. MARK Or you'd wave at each other. I did it today, I was driving around downtown Kenosha, and it was a four-door, nothing special, but that's OK, He, how you doing? Yeah I still flash my headlights at people. (Muniz and O'Guinn 2001: 422)

Saab drivers also passed along stories that became captured in commercials about harrowing, near-death experiences. The Saab's superior performance "saved" the consumer's life. Remain faithful to the brand and see salvation – a religious imagery with deep resonance. The brand takes on sacred-like qualities as protection totems, and loyalty to the brand has religious-like qualities of salvation and redemption.

Rituals bring consumers together, helping consumers realize the benefits to brand loyalty, and drawing them closer to people like themselves, while at the same time enabling them to define themselves as unlike a set of undesirable people. As individuals engage one another in their social networks, their circuits of commercial (and non-commercial) exchange, and in their ritual-like patterns of interaction, they generate and maintain their tastes for goods.

Accidents of History and Market Demand

Outside of rituals, accidents of history matter. Economic sociologists and historians well know the concept of path dependent development and the modal case of the modern keyboard. When economic historians refer to path dependence, they mean that a person or an organization's conduct or the course of action being taken persists as a result of those actions becoming ingrained over time. Although better options become available or other courses of action are feasible, they are not pursued. Past decisions and behaviors create inertia.

The Cultural Roots of Market Demand

When the keyboard was introduced, the letters Q-W-E-R-T and Y in the upper-left-hand side of the keyboard required typists to slow their speed. The point was not to help typists type as fast as possible in a frictionless environment; instead, it was to help typists avoid having letters get stuck that are too close to one another in the typewriter's carriage. Paul David (1986) recalls the 1860s when typing too quickly led to the keys jamming and typing on a machine which precluded viewing an entire typed sentence before it was completing meant that small mistakes cascaded into larger time consuming problems. Improvements in technology made other letter arrangements more efficient than the ones found on the QWERTY keyboard, but these improved technologies did not find an eager set of consumers ready to abandon techniques and work habits that had become ingrained. Economic historian Brian Arthur (1989) observed that the demand for the QWERTY keyboard had become locked in. Implicit in the QWERTY account is the story of how the demand for a specific type of keyboard depended less on what was most efficient in terms of speed or cost-effective in terms of price.

Path dependent development also results from geopolitics and spectacular societal disruptions. Economic historians have demonstrated that large-scale changes in demand may occur after a nation has gone to war. On the one hand, a war represents a large-scale societal disruption. On the other, it marks the emergence of new economic and political coalitions, as some corporate actors are strengthened but others weakened by the geopolitics of war. Substitutes for restricted goods (such as beer for wine) become the standard rather than the stand-in, and in the case of Britain and France, for example, these changed consumption patterns become viewed as a reflection of national culture. Ironically, after the fact, national culture seems to explain why the British drink beer but the French wine; however, before the fact, national culture may have played only a bit part in the larger drama.

27

The Cultural Roots of Market Demand

Historian John V. C. Nye (2007) argues that the beer and wine drinking stereotypes that seem to define British and French societies, respectively, have resulted from wars and from economic policies, not national culture. Before the Nine Years War and the War of Spanish Succession, the consumption of beer and wine did not differ markedly from one country to the other. During the wars the French could not export their wines to Britain for nearly twenty-five years between 1689 and 1713, and the British responded by developing a new import arrangement with Portugal. These new importing arrangements meant that there were new industries and economic interests on the political scene. To protect their interests, British brewers and distillers as well as the importers of Port from Portugal lobbied to have high duties imposed on French wines, forcing the French to export only its highest quality (and highest priced) wines to Britain, leaving the British beer manufacturers to overtake the mass domestic market. In the 1700s, the British imported less than 5 percent of the volume of French wine than it had in the 1600s. As the Industrial Revolution took hold in Britain, the emerging middle class found its alcoholic tastes focused on beer, port, and gin; without the wars and the economic policies aimed at French wine, the stereotypical tastes of the British might have been otherwise. Their political economies, not their national cultures, shaped national taste trends. Once these trends came into existence, it seemed self-evident that these preferences were choices freely made rather than the unanticipated outcomes of two protracted wars as well as the emergent goal of political lobbyists.

Richard Peterson and N. Anand (2004: 315) also emphasize how government policies, in this case copyright laws, affect national tastes. They draw from Wendy Griswold's (1981) study of American and British novels to explain that in the nineteenth century the tastes of American novelists for man-against-nature themes and the contrasting tastes of British novelists for its emphases on proper manners may have had less to do with the national cultures they inhabited than with the laws and regulations governing the publishing industry. This production of culture perspective emphasizes restrictions on certain types of publications by virtue of different copyright arrangements. American novelists received royalties for each book sold while British novelists received a flat fee. Although both the Americans and the British may have started writing the same kinds of novels, the Americans soon found that their copyright arrangements made their books more expensive and comparatively less desirable for their publics compared with the cheaper British novels. The Americans responded by seeking out a niche in subject area as a response to the disadvantages imposed on them by copyright law. These copyright laws had unintended consequences for the types of novels being written in the two countries as readers and distributors (publishers) evaluated the different costs of these cultural goods. And these suppliers restricted what was available to readers in the United States versus Britain. Readers fell in love with what was available, but a supply-side phenomenon became taken as a deeply cultural response to the reading material itself.

Similarly, Michael Schudson has identified the First World War as a key event leading to the rapid rise in demand for cigarettes, but Schudson focuses on how military policies extracted young men from their homes and placed them in tight-knit groups overseas rather than how economic policies might have restricted a competing good from vying for the soldiers' attention. Simply stated, when the United States went to war, its soldiers began smoking cigarettes; when they returned to civilian life, they continued to smoke (Schudson 1984). While the decision to go to war by a nation-state is not to increase the number of cigarette smokers in its population, war nonetheless led to the unanticipated and, for the nation-state, unrecognized outcome.

These studies of path-dependence deal with goods characterized by their inelastic demand curves. According to the

Oxford English Dictionary (second online edition), inelastic demand refers to consumption patterns that "vary less than in proportion to changes in price." In other words, when prices increase for a good or service, the quantity demanded does not decline as much as would be expected in response to the price increase. In fact, there is almost no change in the quantity of the good or service consumed. Economists do not study the source of inelastic demand but rather the small effect of price increases on quantity reductions characterizing such demand functions. Examples: tobacco, alcohol, gambling, health care (life-threatening), things that people have become addicted to (physical need), and goods or services lacking substitutes (scarcity of options). By contrast, elastic demand refers to the change in the quantity of a good or service consumed as a positive and proportionate function of the change in price of the good or service. In other words, as the good or service becomes more expensive, the quantity of consumption decreases accordingly.

Path dependent demand usually describes the characteristics of relatively inelastic demand patterns that emerge over time and that become locked-in. Lock-in patterns may also emerge for goods and services exhibiting elastic demand characteristics; however, the greater the length of exposure to the practice of using a good or service, the more likely the demand for the practice exhibits inertia. This means that lock-in effects will be more easily identifiable and more plentiful for inelastic than for elastic demand. National culture may well explain differences in preferences for some goods from one country to the next, but path dependent development emphasizes what particular people and groups do as a creative response or a defensive reaction to the political, economic, and social circumstances they face. Path dependent explanations pinpoint when large-scale social, political, and economic changes occurred as well as how local and national actors responded to these changes and to one another, sometimes muddling through, improvising, and taking new courses of action as opportunities permit.

Marketing, Manipulation, and Market Demand

Writing in the *American Journal of Sociology* in 1928, Edward Bernays proposed that strategic action on the part of organizations could sway consumer demand. The savvy manipulator paid attention to basic human motives of consumers (survival, sex/reproduction, and love), the constellation of stakeholders (businesses, suppliers, distributors, potential allies, potential opponents), the physical means of communicating with the intended audience (radio, newspapers, the movie, the letter, the stage), and the social sources of authority, charisma, and cleavage. Managing all of these elements, one could sway the general public to like some goods more than others.

Some social conventions that seem to have emerged *ex nihilo* turn out to be the consequences of consumer manipulation. Writing about Edward Bernays and the birth of "spin," journalist Larry Tye portrays the rise of what many restaurant menus around the world call "The American Breakfast" as an attempt to increase bacon sales rather than a manifestation of culturally based eating habits. Tye (1998: 51) writes:

> In the mid-1920s a huge bacon producer, Beechnut Packing Company, hired [Edward] Bernays to help restore sales that had sagged as a country on the run trimmed its morning meal to juice, toast, and coffee ... Bernays resolved to transform America's eating habits. He persuaded a famous New York doctor to write his colleagues asking whether they supported hearty or light breakfasts. Hearty won big, newspapers spread the word, people followed their physicians' advice, and sales soared of the two items most identified with big breakfasts – bacon and eggs.

Bernays understood the importance of legitimate authority provided by physicians and the fact that self-interests such as provisioning for one's household can only be understood in relation to what one perceives others to be doing. Although the previous provisions of a lighter breakfast seemed to work fine for most families, their revealed preference for particular types of breakfast foods could only be understood in relation to what they thought people-like-themselves ought to do to protect and provide for their household. Moreover, a new practice emerged in which "four out of five" doctors or dentists endorse a particular brand. The sources of authority for the various products include the American Dental Society, the American Cancer Society, and the American Heart Association – professional groups presumably more concerned about people's health than about the profitability of a brand.

To show how to manipulate demand based on other forms of authority, Bernays (1928) describes how the buying habits of women had shifted from felt to velvet, silk, and straw hats. As Bernays examined the social structure of female hat users, he found that they constituted four groups: "the society leader" (traditional and charismatic authority), "the style expert" (rational expertise/ bureaucratic authority), "the artist" (quasi-religious/ transcendental authority), and socially recognized "beautiful" women (the reference group). Any strategy to change what women hat users want to consume must contend with the constellation of hat users and their sources of legitimacy. Bernays called upon a distinguished society leader from one of America's leading families, an expert from *Condé Nast* and *Vogue*, a sculptor by the name of Leo Lentelli, and a female model whose image would be distinct for each hat-type. The means deployed included events with a French Countess or Duchess and French couturiers (traditional authority); an exhibit of American silks at the Louvre (transcendental authority); a fashion reporter in the American newspaper (rational authority); and stock characters pictured in the workshops of the dressmakers and hat makers (reference group). As intended, the purchase of velvet hats increased.

When Douglas Holt takes up the question of socially constructing demand, he focuses on the iconic branding. An iconic brand is a brand that has become a cultural icon. He distinguishes these from identity brands – "vessels of self-expression […] imbued with stories that consumers find valuable in constructing their identities" (Holt 2004: 3) – such as Reebok, Pepsi, Saab, Coors, IBM, and Dewars, etc.; instead he focuses on such brands that have become cultural icons as Apple, Nike, Harley Davidson, Coke, and Bud that "become consensus expressions of particular values held dear by some members of society" (Holt 2004: 4). Some product brands become iconic as social and cultural conditions make them resonant in some time-periods but not others (Holt 2004). Iconic brands resonate because they address *cultural disruptions* in society.

> Budweiser became the most desirable beer in the 1980s because the brand addressed one of the most acute contradictions of the day. Working men were motivated by Ronald Reagan's battle cry as he invoked America's frontier myth to restore the country's economic might. The country's economic and political meltdown in the 1970s, along with the increasing independence of women, had left them feeling emasculated. Reagan's call to arms gave these workers hope that they would soon regain their lost manhood. These same men, however, were beginning to realize that their vocations as skilled manual laborers, their primary source of masculine identity, were becoming obsolete as these jobs were replaced by technology and outsourced overseas. Budweiser targeted this acute tension between the revived American ideals of manhood and the economic realities that made these ideals nearly unattainable for many men. (Holt 2004: 6–7)

As marketers explicitly consider these cultural disruptions (or somehow feel them in their gut), they come to understand what types of myths are emerging to deal with the gap between the ideal and the current realities. As a result of these society-wide disruptions, what Holt calls a myth market has the power to resonate with consumers.

For Holt, myth markets encapsulate (1) collective narratives about what kind of nation one inhabits (national identity)

(2) what types of disruptions in society have rendered some myths as necessary and others as implausible, and (3) what the existing activities are among non-commercial worlds such as sports, music, and popular art where groups of people seem motivated by their sincere commitments and beliefs rather than by the need to profit from a product (populist worlds). Advertisers pay attention to these three components of myth markets, recognizing that it is in the populist worlds where sincerity is prized that an iconic brand will be (partially) authored and judged. In other words, a consumer can see that there are voluntary groups of people who are not being paid by an advertiser to use a product, but who use a product religiously, sometimes ostentatiously, and are willing to defend vigorously the product's virtues.

To make myth markets concrete, Holt offers the example of how PepsiCo promoted the Mountain Dew brand. Mountain Dew advertisements relied on three myths: the hillbilly myth of the 1950s and 60s drew on images from the popular L'il Abner cartoon and from the widely watched television show *The Beverly Hillbillies*. After cultural disruptions in the late 1960s (i.e. urban unrest, Watergate, and Vietnam), the redneck myth emerged as images from the television program *The Dukes of Hazzard* showed two men defying their corrupt local sheriffs, having fun, and being free. Another set of cultural disruptions (i.e. scandals on Wall Street; entrepreneurial dreams called into question) in the late 1980s gave way to the slacker myth with the detachment from reality of *Wayne's World* and the physical engagement and personal victories being portrayed in the newly popular extreme sports. By the 1990s, PepsiCo announced its position on what lay at the core of its advertising strategy for Mountain Dew: "To 18-year-old males, who embrace excitement, adventure and fun, Mountain Dew is the great tasting carbonated soft drink that exhilarates like no other because it is energizing, [is] thirst-quenching, and has a one-of-a-kind citrus flavor" (Holt 2004: 64).

The Cultural Roots of Market Demand

Unlike marketers who focus on cultural disruptions and myths in order to identify what types of images and stories will encourage consumers to revere and buy specific products, Juliet Schor hones in on the intrusive forms of research that identify how children use products, what types of games they play with them, and how children use their consumption to feel as if they are worthy of participating in their preferred social groups. Schor describes a researcher who is visiting a five-year-old girl and has a video camera in order to capture everything that she possibly can about how this five-year-old experiences health and beauty products.

> [A] health and beauty aids company with a bubble bath product [...] wants to explore Caitlin's [a five-year-old girl] feelings about bath time and learn what she actually does while she's bathing. After some talk, Caitlin leads [Mary] Prescott [who is a New York advertising executive] and her camera into the bathroom, where Mary spies a shelf full of empty shampoo and bubble bath bottles. She learns that Caitlin plays with them during her bath, which leads to the consumer insight that kids turn soap containers into toys. Prescott explains that had she done the research in a focus group facility or even in the kitchen, she wouldn't have happened upon the empty containers. (Schor 2004: 99)

As marketers have taken the ethnographic turn, they have been able to observe at close range how children and other consumers use products. Rather than rely solely on what consumers say they do with products, advertising researchers have tried to capture the things that consumers take for granted – the games they play, the things they hang in the closet, the way they assign importance to a favorite blouse relative to other tops on the rack, and even the things they carry and use on their school playgrounds and in their cafeterias.

This form of intrusive ethnographic research by advertising companies, Schor tells us, began in the 1980s. The Levi Strauss jeans company wanted to know what young people were putting in their closets. Rather than dictate what's cool or what's desirable, Levi Strauss first wanted to know how ordinary people were rating the value of their clothes. Levis demonstrated how one could search for what is cool, then redesign one's existing product-line based on what one found. The feedback loop is a dynamic one, with consumers making adjustments based on the redesigns, sending the marketers and their client companies back to the drawing board.

Even with the feedback loop, Schor warns, advertisers nonetheless induced new forms of consumption through savvy messaging and by tapping influential opinion setters for children. Companies placed advertisements for junk food prominently in cartoons, movies, and other programs popular with children. Hershey's, for example, created a Kidztown, and a number of companies have provided schools with funds and new curricula bearing their logos. Even as children squawk from the cradle, they are being targeted; therefore, it should come as no surprise that by the time an American child enters kindergarten, she can recognize about 300 commercial logos, and by the age of ten, the names of 400 brands.

Even the way that children navigate through department stores has been manipulated to increase their demand for the store's products. Daniel Thomas Cook has described this process in *The Commodification of Childhood* (2004). He describes the layout of department stores, and notes how younger children would have to walk through the sections where the older children found their clothes. This orderly progression of age categories meant that the youngest children could imagine themselves progressing as consumers. Younger children worship older ones, and they strive to grow up quickly, so that they can be like the older, stronger, faster kids. Before the layout of the stores changed to induce demand among children, mothers would find that the clothing they needed for their youngest children was located conveniently near their own clothing section. Little walking needed to be done, and children were not seen as consumers. To generate a consumer identity, the spatial layout of the store had to be manipulated.

Even before advertisers were interviewing children and trying to think about how they experience retail spaces, historian William Leach found that department stores kept their eyes on rituals and special celebrations that people used to mark annual (recurring), special events. The floor displays provided justifications for special purchases made for these special moments; this was not spending done on a whim. The passage of each season seemed to be marked in one way or another, so the department stores found a way to "reritualiz[e] the passage of time" (Leach 1984: 322) by changing their floor displays for Thanksgiving, Christmas, Hanukkah, and Easter. In 1924, Macy's department store sponsored a Thanksgiving Day Parade that its immigrant employees organized. The parade persists.

What made the manipulation of demand so effective was its linkage with functions and activities that did not have economic profits as their goals. These functions included child care, free art exhibitions, free public lectures, free plays, free concerts, anthropological displays and public library branches aimed at education. Leach captures the irony of a profit machine with "non-profit" motives:

> Over time many Americans had come to consider the department store as an "eleemosynary [charitable] institution maintained for the purpose of serving the public without regard for profit" ... As an English advertising manager from Harrods in London declared in 1919, "I do not know whether stores have created and fostered the demand for service which department stores recognized and met; but it certainly causes a tremendous amount of overhead expense, and it is a question if it has not been carried too far." (Leach 1984: 330)

Indeed, John Wanamaker founded one of the first department store chains in the United States (absorbed by Hecht's, then Macy's). He referred to the Wanamaker department store as "the people's store" after professing his belief that the stores motive to provide services to the public trumped its drive for economic profits, so when its women workers began to participate in the suffrage movement, the store allowed them to march on company time and sold the movement's clothing and other paraphernalia through its stores. The commercial venture allied itself with the goals of liberty and reframed its activities as reflecting freedom. Had the department store not done this, social movements may have come to see the consumerism that these stores promote as targets for social change. To maintain consumer demand for goods, department stores framed themselves as apolitical venues where a spirit of liberty and public service reigned.

At the point of purchase, Sharon Zukin (2004) finds consumers mesmerized by goods. Although manipulated by marketers, buyers are nonetheless establishing who they are (identity work) as they select the right type of shops for people-like-themselves. Going shopping is a social adventure, conducted with family members or friends. The lessons of how to be a smart shopper and how to be a savvy dresser are civic lessons; the opportunity for mothers to shop with their daughters offers quality time for bonding and for passing along stories and lessons about good behavior and common courtesy.

According to George Ritzer, consumer culture has responded to the disenchantment that would have come had there been a complete rationalization of social life as the capitalist market commodified everything in its path. To combat the disenchantment that would have spelled doom for capitalism, suppliers of goods have rationally and deliberately recreated the magical, sacred, and sometimes religious character of social life in places of consumption.

> The new means of consumption can be seen as "cathedrals of consumption" – that is, they are structured, often successfully, to have an enchanted, sometimes even sacred, religious character.

To attract ever-larger numbers of consumers, such cathedrals of consumption need to offer, or at least appear to offer, increasingly magical, fantastic, and enchanted settings in which to consume ... A worker involved in the opening of McDonald's in Moscow spoke of it "as if it were the Cathedral in Chartres... a place to experience 'celestial joy.'" A visit to Disney World has been depicted as "the middle-class hajj, the compulsory visit to the sunbaked city," and analogies have been drawn between a trip to Disney World and pilgrimages to religious sites such as Lourdes. (Ritzer 1999: 7)

The stores themselves have become icons. Creative energies focus on the re-enchantment of commodities and the buying experience. The consumer, in Ritzer's telling, is a cultural dupe who follows a fake hope that these cathedrals of consumption will not wipe out authentic islands of cultural expression.

Accounting for Tastes

Behavioral psychologists have also undertaken studies of consumer demand, largely to evaluate the mental shortcuts and informal rules that govern purchase decisions. Richard Thaler (1999), Amos Tversky, and Daniel Kahneman (1981) are some of the most well known psychologists addressing these questions. They hone in on the decisions that seem to make little sense for a rationally calculating person with enough information to make an informed choice. Much of their research falls under the heading of prospect theory (e.g. Tversky and Kahneman 1981).

Let's take the example of expected losses and expected gains. A financial loss followed by a mathematically equivalent gain should yield a net of zero, but the consumer experiences losses and gains differently and prefers a gain to a loss. This means that winning the lottery twice but gaining 500 dollars each time is preferred to winning once and gaining 1,200 but losing 200 the second time. These two lottery scenarios are mathematically equivalent. In the first instance, the expected gain is 1,000; in the second instance, it is also 1,000. But when most people are asked what they would prefer, and they largely line up behind winning twice. Some would even prefer to win twice and make a little less than a 1,000, if this means that they could avoid a loss.

Behavioral psychologists have also confirmed insights found in Viviana Zelizer's work, namely that people earmark money differently according to how it was earned and by whom. This earmarked money gets used for different purposes and can be spent frugally or frivolously, not out of consideration of what the total budget of the household is or what the household needs are, but rather as a function of how the money is earmarked. Money earned by a child who mows lawns on the weekend is probably spent on school clothes but not on the electric bill. Money coming into the family coffers from a lottery ticket or a tax refund will be spent differently than will money coming in from a father's salary. Money earned from a conference honorarium will be spent more freely than will funds coming from an inheritance, and so on.

Individuals evaluate their purchase of goods and services relative to a norm rather than an absolute satisfaction standard. The norm is socially established and culturally interpreted. The preference function does not inhere solely in the individual or in an asocial calculation of price relative to quantity. More importantly, an individual's preference for a good or service depends in part on the social meaning of the purchase (frivolous versus prudent), the frequency with which the individual usually makes the purchase, and the source of the funds. Windfall gains are more likely to be used for frivolous purchases; money earned on a regular and predictable basis will be diverted to more essential purchases. In short, the revealed preference of the consumer will depend on how she obtained the funds for the purchase and the social meanings imbued in the purchase.

These mental accounts are thoroughly embedded in social and cultural meaning structures. Thaler highlights the difference between acquisition and transaction utility in order to demonstrate how the revealed preference for a good or service depends on the social context of consumption. If an individual is willing to pay five dollars for a beer at a fancy resort, that same individual should be willing to pay five dollars for a beer in another venue, if one only focused on acquisition utility. If focused on the transaction utility, however, the individual would evaluate the reference price of the beer as being appropriate or inappropriate for a particular social setting. The revealed preference of the individual depends on her particular desire for a good, its price, and the meaningful context in which the good is purchased and consumed. One can hardly understand the demand for goods and services without understanding the timing of the purchase decision, the actual payment for goods and services rendered, and the anticipation of benefits to be accrued after initial consumption.

Different meanings of the purchase utility emerge in different temporalities. The timing of payment, rebates, and bonuses influences consumer demand by tempering losses and heightening gains. In a hedonic framing, demand increases when a small gain temporally follows a larger loss; and in prospect theory, the evaluation of the purchase depends on consumer's reference point, itself a socially oriented benchmark: a rebate arrives as confirmation that one's desire for a good or service coincided with a price structure considered by oneself and one's peer group as advantageous. The evaluation of price is a relational process, in which the temporality and the segregation of gains and losses affect how the price is evaluated – a sacrifice too great or a relatively small pain followed in time by relief (a cash rebate). It is the culture of money that makes it worthwhile, that generates various justifications for its use, and that keeps consumers engaged with one another (in the flesh or in spirit) as they think about what they want and how much they are willing to sacrifice to get it.

Even the way one evaluates altruism, what should be given gratis for what one should be paid, depends on cultural logics about money (see more about this in Chapter 4). In *Last Best Gifts*, for example, Kieran Healy describes the complex transactions that made donating blood an altruistic act. Altruism depends on the transaction media being exchanged and the narratives attached to the transaction defining the situation as altruistic. People who declared themselves organ donors, for example, received a discount on their insurance premium, a form of payment that did not get in the way of the donor holding on to a narrative of being good without being paid for it. In states like Pennsylvania where cash payments could be made for organ donation, the payments were earmarked as gifts to the funeral home to assist with the cost of the funeral for the deceased. New names, stories, and transaction rituals did not merely disguise payments but transformed them from an instrument of commensuration in an a-cultural market to a meaningful object that facilitates exchange, bolsters meanings, and that gets used in defining situations and things as sacred.

Conclusion

To conclude, sociologists have a great deal to say about the culture of market demand. This chapter has offered an introduction to the cultural studies explaining the importance of shared meanings for a person's decision to consume goods and how those purchase decisions are accounted for. Market demand is not simply the aggregation of lots of individuals who just happen to like or to dislike similar things; instead, market demand reflects processes that generate meaning and that assert a sense of belonging to a group. Anyone who has tried to sell a product or to keep a company afloat should recognize the insights in this chapter to be plausible, if not directly relevant to the day-to-day, dynamic, and unfolding decisions that are made about how to appeal to a specific demographic, how to use social ties or group rituals to promote a brand, or how to change the way that a person thinks about her purchase so that she can justify spending greater and greater sums. While this chapter is not exhaustive in its coverage of all the available studies on culture and consumer demand, it should prove sufficient for launching readers toward the next, closely coupled topic of market supply.

2

The Cultural Dimensions of Market Supply

Textbook understandings of markets conceal the meaningful, sometimes confusing, realm in which the suppliers of goods and services operate. When a supplier is not following a textbook pattern of behavior, especially when there seems to be a methodical approach to just how off the "model" the supplier's behavior is, most people assume that this could only be happening in a foreign country that has not yet learned how to be properly capitalist or that is undergoing a transition toward American-style capitalism; however, thoughtful analysts understand that some of the same dynamics found among companies in other countries and in other economic systems are manifest in companies studied in the United States. In *The Sense of Dissonance*, economic sociologist David Stark recalls his own realization that much of what he had observed in other countries was happening in places like Silicon Valley. Stark writes about his time as a Visiting Fellow at the Center for Advanced Study in the Behavioral Sciences in Palo Alto in the mid-to-late 1990s and how the realization came to him while on the sidelines of a soccer field.

> I was watching my daughter's soccer practice … and struck up a conversation with another parent. He was curious about my research in Hungarian firms and asked me to describe what I had

been finding. "Well, I sometimes have difficulty knowing where one firm ends and another one begins," I began. He nodded encouragement to continue. I went on to mention the blurring of public and private and then how firms sometimes collaborate on projects without getting all the property arrangements settled at the outset. At each step he kept me going with an encouraging "Yeah, and...?" After four or five such promptings, he interrupted, "You're not talking about Hungary. You're talking about Silicon Valley." (Stark 2009: xv)

From one industry to the next, there are different understandings about how business should be done and there are difference practices that loosely match those understandings. David Stark finds that people within companies evaluate the steps they take using a range of scales and evaluative criteria. They tell stories about the things they did that count and the things that happened that did not count (or that should not count). These modes of accounting help them assess what to produce, when, how, and at what costs (in terms of money, materials, status, and principles).

This notion of suppliers as complex organizations engaged in consequential storytelling stands in stark contrast to the rather textbook depiction of supply curves that aggregate how much (quantity) each company in a given sector is willing to produce at a particular price. In the standard version of market supply, companies minimize their costs and maximize their revenue using the optimal technologies at their grasp. The market price results from the coincidence of the suppliers' willingness to produce and the buyers' willingness to purchase the aggregate quantity of goods or services at a mutual (market) price. What David Stark and other economic sociologists have found, however, is that the willingness to produce a good or service at a particular price is not merely a technical outcome evaluated along a single measure. As a result, businesses sometimes do things that seem to have little to do with maximizing profits.

The Cultural Dimensions of Market Supply

This chapter outlines why companies do the things they do and why industries vary in how they are organized. In order to see clearly the cultural dynamics at play, we will largely bracket questions about how long a company has been in operation and what its structural attributes are. And when we do mention these seemingly non-cultural aspects of businesses, we will argue that the standard structural attributes are shaped by the way that people are able to evaluate (see) opportunities versus threats, understanding some actions to be appropriate and in the realm of the possible but other (technically feasible alternatives) to be out of the question. This will lead us to address three themes.

(1) The cultural history of a nation or an industry matters for the opportunities that business people will be able to "see" as viable for them. Cultural history refers to the narratives, symbols, and shared understandings that help people evaluate what ought to be produced and how (institutional logics); and these cultural histories form a public culture or an industrial culture in which companies operate.

(2) Organizational cultures emerge from rituals and stories. These organizational cultures provide individuals with "rules" for how to behave within the organization, criteria for evaluating performances including but not exclusive to economic profit making, and a specialized language and style of operation marking members of the organization's tribe as being distinct from those outside of the organization or the organizational clique.

(3) How we categorize actions, persons, and things is not merely a reflection of reality but is a force that acts on reality. Definitions about what type of work someone is doing has consequences for how that work will be received in the marketplace; likewise, definitions about what type of worker a person is has implications for how that person can participate in labor markets.

These cultural dimensions of market supply help us understand some of the puzzles raised in the book's introduction. Why are railroads and healthcare organized differently in countries that have the same access to information and technology? Why does the charisma of the company's leader or the generation of "tribal" loyalty matter in a highly rationalized organization? Why does the sense of morality that people have when they are operating on behalf of a company seem to differ dramatically from the way they talk about morality outside of their role within the company? And why does the ethical sense of right and wrong and the logic of civic good still find their way into the operations of these complex, bureaucratic, rationalized organizations?

Cultural Histories and Logics of Action

Entire industries have institutional logics governing how decisions are made within companies. Patricia Thornton and William Ocasio (1999) have investigated, for example, how an institutional logic focused on editorial issues versus one focused on market issues affects how executives within higher education publishing houses are promoted. Whereas the mission of the publisher is to build the prestige of the house and to increase the sales volume under an editorial logic; under a market logic the mission changes to building the house's competitive position and increasing its profits. According to an executive at one of the publishing houses, the editorial logic worked something like this.

> Nobody talked about profits; sales, yes, but not profits ... A lot of the publishing companies in those days were still run by the grand old men of publishing. I used to see Mr Knopf come in every day with his white hair and his cane and walk into his dark blue velvet office with a great mahogany desk. There were truly devoted editors, who were really into literature... And so this world was

really not about business, and nobody cared that much about making a lot of money. You went into publishing because you liked authors and books. (quoted in Thornton and Ocasio 1999: 809)

The editors are legends; the settings in which they work, legendary. The meaning of the work was about the ideas and the power of the written word. Economic profits were an afterthought. These industry logics carry with them stories about what each house holds as sacred and against what types of behaviors the sacred has had to be protected.

In the 1980s, however, the institutional logics began to change. Building personal imprints gave way to building market channels, and the personal reputation of the editors became less of a concern for the house's legitimacy compared with the house's market position. According to Heather Haveman and Hayagreeva "Huggy" Rao (2006), such shifts in institutional logics come as a result of large-scale changes in society. Not only is there more competition within an industry and new technologies that threaten an existing institutional logic, but often the social connections that people had begin to change with consequences for the maintenance of an existing logic, and new understandings of legitimacy emerge.

Stephen Barley and Gideon Kunda trace how management discourse changes from one time-period to the next. These large-scale shifts in how business leaders talked about their mission reflect changing cultural dynamics pulled between the normative and the rational. By normative, the authors refer to the social obligations that the captains of industry felt they had to the societies in which they operated; by rational, the authors refer to the emphasis on scientific management principles, pushing aside social obligations for coldly calculated ends. Religious reasoning became intertwined with profitability logics in the 1800s. In the 1870s, Washington Gladden, a prominent Congregationalist minister, preached that the moral and mental qualities of workers would be improved as a consequence of the working for large industries.

> So long as the wage system prevails... employers of labor will be, to some degree, responsible for the well-being of the mechanics and operatives. The power that wealth gives them ... is a power that carries with it heavy obligations ... First among them is the obligation to care for the physical health and comfort of his work-people ... The Christian law is, that we are to do good to all men as we have the opportunity; and certainly the employer's opportunity is among his employees. (Barley and Kunda 1992: 367)

This normative ideology of industrial betterment lasted from about 1870 to 1900. By emphasizing the duties that people have to one another, the discourse of industrial betterment placed a great deal of responsibility for the health and education of employees on the backs of the factory owners and managers.

Then came the rationalist discourse (1900–23) exemplified by Frederick Taylor. In his quest to improve factory productivity, he focused not on how people's lives could be improved, but rather on the bottom line of profit and profitability. He reviled social welfare programs and thought of self-respecting working people to be willing to embrace progress (scientific management) and to be averse to government handouts. The rational rhetoric, however, gave way to normative notions of human relations and welfare capitalism from about 1925 to 1955; switching back to a rational discourse of systems management with operations research and management science (1955–80), and then back to a normative emphasis on organizational culture (starting in the 1980s).

The bipolar swings in management discourse indicate that there is a cultural structure with the normative and the rational serving as the opposite ends of the rhetorical spectrum. Recognizing this dualism, Barley and Kunda acknowledge the work of structural anthropologists and the role of oppositional concepts at the structure's core: "In preindustrial societies, pivotal dualisms often encode naturalistic and religious enigmas: life versus death, good versus evil, and so on. Most anthropologists agree that although industrial cultures are less dualistic than preindustrial cultures, oppositions still continue to play a crucial role" (385).

Frank Dobbin explains the variation in industrial policy in the United States, Britain, and France as a cultural phenomenon. During the railway age, these countries had access to the same technology, yet each chose a different path for organizing its railway system. Why did the rational actors in these modern, Western countries not "see" (frame) their industrial policies in the same way after receiving the same information and technology about how the railway could be forged? The answer lies in culture.

Dobbin explains how a country's political culture guides economic policy by noting what types of industrial policies would be out of the question in the United States but taken as a given in France: "Why does the United States always use antitrust law to govern industries, whereas Frances always uses proactive state coordination? [...] What are the chances that the United States will, as France sometimes does, designate the industry a 'national champion' and use public monies to turn it into a monopoly? Take any odds against it" (Dobbin 1994: 11). In other words, to understand the political culture in which policymakers operate is to understand why they perceive some options as possibilities but others as far-fetched.

Industrial culture is "the institutionalized principles of industrial organization and economic behavior found within countries. Being cultural, they consist of practices and associated meaning" (Dobbin 1994: 18). And political culture consists in how situations are understood as problematic and what set of actions are deemed appropriate for particular types of problems. Dobbin demonstrates the power of political culture by illustrating how its variation led to rather different outcomes in the United States, Britain, and France:

> [I]n the United States and Britain, political institutions reinforced community and individual sovereignty, respectively, and guarded against the concentration of political power in the central state. In the emergent industrial economy, these countries viewed community and individual *economic self-determination* as integral to *economic order*, and guarded against the concentration of economic power in the state and in private enterprises. France, with political structures designed to achieve order by concentrating authority, perceived concentrated economic authority as a means to economic order and thus chartered huge regional railway monopolies that operated under close state supervision. (Dobbin 1994: 20)

The perception of economic order in these three countries comes from each country's experience of organizing their militaries and other government agencies to maintain order. These organizing strategies became blueprints for handling other non-political problems.

In Britain, political order comes from the sovereignty imbued in the individual: "The legislature had been the forum in which men of substance who ruled the nation's 'parcelized sovereignties' decided their common fate" (Dobbin 1994: 163). Just as the state protected individual elites from their neighbors and from the Crown in political life, it performed the same operation in economic life. The state protected weak passengers, employees, and small firms, even as it exalted individual entrepreneurs. The state did not offer public financing for the railways as it followed the principle of laissez-faire, epitomized in the writings of Adam Smith. The area where policymakers perceived a public problem was in protecting the rights of landowners and investors, and the state's history of land enclosures and its defining of some investor actions as incurring on the rights of their neighboring investors made their actions make sense in their political culture.

In France, rule or law constitutes political order, and a central authority guarantees it. Such ordering principles have consequences. The financial means to develop the railway system lay in the hands of the state because French banks did not have much experience loaning large sums of money to entrepreneurs for these types of ventures. It made sense that such undertakings would be built through public finance. Having a set of expert technocrats make railway policy offered freedom for all. The technocrats (like priests) would study the scriptures and would do what was right.

By imposing stringent requirements for private sector participation in railway construction and controlling the process from a central authority, the technocrats ensured that those who truly believed in serving the nation's goals (along with those who stubbornly insisted on being part of the process) would join in service. When problems with corruption came to light, in France it was interpreted as the result of too little state regulation; however, across the Atlantic, the same problem was interpreted as the inevitable result of too much state meddling.

In the United States, community self-rule represented political order, but centralized political authority represented its opposite. Such principles of order sometimes ruled even when practical problems might have required their relaxation. For example, in the 1860s each railway had its own gauge rather than a standard gauge across railways, making the diverse railways incompatible. It was better to let the markets work freely than to standardize the gauges from a government-run, central authority. A private sector solution emerged as a private company worked to convince all the railway industries to use a standard gauge. In this case, the actors did not seek the most efficient solution to handling the problem of inconsistent gauge sizes. Instead, they pursued the types of solutions *that made sense for their political culture.*

These binaries line up with Jeffrey Alexander and Philip Smith's (2003) discussion of the sacred and the profane, with the former representing order, the latter disorder; the former, the good; the latter, the bad. Rather than regulation, the ordering principles in the United States encouraged more competition. Dobbin describes how the stances taken by policymakers in the United States changed over time as they tinkered with how to improve safety and what to do about cartels. Policymakers are not cultural dupes who blindly follow ordering principles, but these principles provide the touchstone for decisions that veer away. Regulation requires justification narratives that acknowledge the principles to be protected, that laments (with a contrite heart) the inability to comply fully with those principles, and that vows to return to them as soon as practically possible.

Nicole Woolsey Biggart and Mauro Guillén (1999) use the concepts of cultural logics and social organization to reformulate the theory of comparative advantage. Firms within countries do not respond in the same way to their own material endowments, the human capital of their workforce, or available technologies. From one country to the next, understandings differ with regard to how these endowments should be used and who may legitimately use them. Biggart and Guillén demonstrate how these logics work by comparing four countries – South Korea, Taiwan, Spain, and Argentina – that tried to enter the automobile assembly and component manufacturing sector after the Second World War. These countries acted as if one-size-would-fit-all, employing the same development policies but experiencing rather different development outcomes. One can understand these differences in outcome by attending to the local histories of political and industrial development along with the interpretive prisms (logics) through which these industrial policies were refracted (also see Biggart and Orrú 1997).

To understand why institutional logics are so consequential, consider the differences they make for how businesses raise capital. In some social contexts, one takes for granted that business capital will be obtained from one's family. In other contexts, reliance on family ties appears unseemly, so building ties with banks and foreign investors becomes a more "suitable" strategy. These and other practices hold across a given society, not because of the "objective" outcomes or because of "rational" assessments regarding what types of inputs should produce a given set of outcomes. Instead, the actor's notion of what is possible, efficacious, and legitimate shape her strategies of action, and they are aware that others within their social circle may consider them illegitimate or ignorant if they fail to honor these strategies (see Biggart and Guillén 1999: 725).

The authors compare two countries that have succeeded in auto-assembly – South Korea and Spain – with two that have not – Taiwan and Argentina. Each country attempted to do the same thing but in a different institutional context where industrial policies defined and dealt with the challenges of industrialization differently and where the *legitimate* categories of actors, relationships, and organizing logics differed. The challenge is not to change the culture of these countries but rather to adjust development strategies so that countries can use their cultural endowments (logics of organization and cultural capabilities) and match them with the most appropriate opportunities offered by the global economy.

Analogously, organizing logics in the health field have consequences for blood donation rates. In the European Union, the health systems all need a strong and steady blood supply, yet there is a great deal of variation in the rate of blood donation, in the types of people who donate blood, and in the blood collection regime from one country to the next. Kieran Healy examines the differences in how blood is collected (government, the Red Cross, and/or blood banks), whether the country has a volunteer donor group, and whether plasma collection centers operate as for-profit. Healy's analysis emphasizes that each country has its own way of seeing what is desirable about one collection regime versus another and that the altruism attributed to an individual's psychological makeup is induced by different organizational settings (Healy 2000: 1634–5). Healy does not, however, tackle why one collection system dominated in country X but another system did so in country Y.

Healy argues that pointing to national cultural differences or to the demographic characteristics of individuals, however, does not explain the variation in blood donation rates. Healy does not examine the political or the industrial cultures the countries in his study; instead, he relies on their geographic proximity and their histories of interaction to make casual comparisons: France and Luxembourg are culturally similar; so too are Denmark and Norway, yet 44 percent of respondents in the 1993 Eurobarometer survey have donated blood in France but only 14 percent in Luxembourg; 34 percent in Denmark, but only 16 percent in Norway (Healy 2000: 1637–8). This weak definition of national culture precludes an analysis of culture as a highly specified variable that structures the collection regimes in each other. Instead, the collection regimes are identified as the real players in the market.

The regimes in the European Union are (1) state run (Britain, France, Ireland), (2) blood banks (Denmark, Greece, Italy, Norway, Portugal, Spain), (3) and the Red Cross (Belgium, Luxembourg, the Netherlands, Germany). In each of these systems, the organizations and the donors themselves define blood donation in rather different ways. To give blood is to engage in voluntary work. Where volunteerism rates are high, so too are rates of blood donation. Likewise, in countries where there is a high rate of church attendance, there is also a high rate of volunteerism; and with greater volunteerism as well as organizations encouraging sacrifice for the good of unknown others, blood donation rates tend to be higher.

Cultural structures also offer semiotic codes against which industries emerge. Take, for example, the producers of grass-fed beef and dairy. Klaus Weber and his colleagues have examined how semiotic codes motivate producers to enter this niche market between 1990 and 2005 (Weber, Heinze, and DeSouzey 2008). The stories that producers tell one another motivate them to enter and to persevere in the niche during the early days when profitability is low and the risks of failure are high. These stories also help the producers develop a collective identity that informs their selection of the appropriate technologies of production for people like themselves.

These logics of appropriateness have deep cultural roots. Margaret Somers and Fred Block highlight the importance of public narratives in their study of government policies and the principles justifying them: "Every nation has a story – a public narrative it tells to explain its place ... in the flow of history, to justify its normative principles, to delineate the boundaries of rational political decisionmaking, and to give meaning to its economic policies and practices" (Somers and Block 2005: 280). I am arguing that these narratives matter for the export strategies of nation-states and their entrepreneurs. In short, the "ideational embeddedness" identified by Somers and Block help us see the social orientation of government export promotion policies. (Chapter 4 will detail the Somers and Block study to demonstrate *how* ideas matter for economic policymaking, rendering some courses of action unthinkable, even when feasible.)

National export platforms enable the display of objects that are themselves stigma or prestige symbols (Wherry 2007, 2008). In *Global Markets and Local Crafts*, Wherry argues that refined objects with narratives of distinction usually represent prestige; raw materials that either require little refinement or whose refinement happens outside of the national territory can represent stigma symbols. The prestige or stigma of exported objects and services do not inhere in the objects or services themselves. Historical narratives and on-the-ground performances make them so.

Some countries have a diverse set of stigma and prestige symbols in their basket of exports. Countries in the economic core of the world-system have the self-confidence and the credibility to take for granted what their export platforms represent because the prestige of those platforms become so closely associated with the nation-state that they seem naturally occurring. However, easily discreditable countries can take little for granted. Too many stigma symbols could doom them to remain in the periphery or could impede their advancement within their class of peers.

Wherry takes the case of handicrafts produced in Thailand and Costa Rica to illustrate how the cultural politics of the state influence what is exported from it. He compares how Thailand and Costa Rica actively participated in the World's Fair with cultural artifacts in the late 1800s, but as the Costa Rican state attempted to present itself as fully assimilated into the Western, industrialized community, it engaged in a campaign of sanitation, cleaning up its indigenous (dirty) elements and emphasizing why the country should deserve the title (later conferred on it by US President Taft) as the Switzerland of Latin America.

By contrast, the Thais were eager to emphasize their cultural distinction, especially as the colonial powers attempted to make claims on territories not culturally bounded to the nation-state. The Thai state delicately orchestrated a selectively acculturated identity, emphasizing its unique symbols and customs while also linking itself to the standards of the West. Fly Thai Airways, for example, and experience cultural uniqueness with Swiss efficiency. These impressions of the country drove policies to assist the promotion of some exports over others, as the country concerned itself with prestige symbols that needed to balance the stigma of raw materials.

How to manage potentially stigmatizing symbols preoccupies various agencies of the nation-state. Lauren Rivera's (2008) study of how Croatia manages stigma in the tourism sector is instructive, advancing the Goffmanian framework sketched in Wherry (2007). She specifies the stigma management strategies country teams engage in, erecting boundaries between themselves and others "unlike" them and establishing linkages with others of higher status that share prestigious characteristics. Presentation teams in the government's tourism authority engage in boundary work (e.g. Lamont and Fournier 1992) to distinguish the country's desirable characteristics from its undesirable ones. The standard for desirability depends on the time-period when Croatia looks more toward the West and after the country's shameful civil war.

Rivera notes that Croatia has three Goffmanian strategies for managing stigma: the country may attempt (1) to cover up the stigma by strategically sending messages, stories, and images to its target audience. This strategy works well if the presentation team has a monopoly over the narrative and if the country's history has elements that can be emphasized (even as disquieting events are silenced) and if the country is not already discredited as an upstanding, believable actor in the global community. Another strategy at its disposal is (2) to embrace the stigma and to reject the norms of its broader audience. This "choice" usually occurs among already discredited actors who feel that they can do little to change outsiders' perceptions. Finally, the presentation team may (3) acknowledge the stigma and can refashion it so that the audience has a favorable impression of the country nonetheless. Acknowledgment strategies usually occur when the presentation team cannot monopolize the narrative about the country's history and its characteristics and where the country itself is either creditable or, if discreditable, not already discredited.

Although she does not explicitly use a Goffmanian framework, Nina Bandelj does acknowledge how stock characters in market dramas are restricted in the parts they are allowed to play. Bandelj develops a relational approach to studying macroeconomic processes and she argues that "culture is consequential because shared collective understandings and meanings shape economic strategies and goals, and affect the interpretations of economic situations" (Bandelj 2008: 4). In her study of Foreign Direct Investment (FDI) in Central and Eastern Europe, she identifies cultural relations between origin and recipient sites as well as political structures, migration, and trade relations to explain why investors focus on some countries but not others, even after controlling for material endowments and demographic attributes. Such a shift in emphasis is not uncommon in microlevel studies of money and intimacy or in craftwork or the cultural industries; however, to take this approach in a macroeconomic study is to take a strong cultural turn that demonstrates how culture has consequences in the macroeconomy. Bandelj offers a strong cultural approach to markets by taking on an area previously thought immune to cultural and social forces.

National identity, Bandelj argues, affects the economic transactions that take place between countries. While recognizing formal institutional structures and political arrangements that affect economic transactions between countries, she also notes how the meanings of national identity influence the types of contacts economic actors from one country will have with actors in another country:

An attempt by an American household appliance manufacturer to buy a majority share in a Slovenian company illustrates [how companies receiving foreign director investment consider the cultural values and practices of the investor before engaging in a long-term partnership]. Perceiving "the American way of doing business" as merciless downsizing and an uncaring attitude toward workers, middle management of the targeted host firm mobilized workers and launched a news campaign against the American investment; labeling it "a hostile take-over" ... As a result, the American firm withdrew the offer because they did not want to be perceived as having negative intentions. Half of this Slovenian company was later acquired by a German multinational whose style of management, due to a history of connections between the two countries, was much more familiar to Slovenes. (Bandelj 2002: 422)

Investors and hosts engage in "cultural matching" as they evaluate whether an exchange partner will be suitable, given the partner's ways of seeing the world. Using this logic, a retired judge explained, "Our office of external affairs would quickly issue all the necessary investment documents to German or Swiss investors, not a problem, but you know, that wouldn't be the case for Italians" (Bandelj 2002: 423).

The way that investors characterize a firm's money and its people are closely tied. Consider the comparison of Germanic people to the Italians:

> Germanic people and Germanic investments are perceived as precise, orderly, trustworthy. Against Italians, there are always some suspicions. That their money is dirty, that things will get messed up, that there is some iffy business involved, that these are unreliable people. While, on the other hand, Germans and Austrians are elevated and treated as hyperorganized, orderly, trustworthy. (Interview, 1 February 2002, quoted in Bandelj 2003: 386)

If a firm views an investor from a particular country to be a good match for a particular category of investment, the firm and its supporting institutions in the host country is more likely to facilitate the match. Otherwise, the match is likely to be blocked, explaining, in part, why some countries with similar structural characteristics may nonetheless find themselves disadvantaged in the global economy relative to their peers.

Mark Granovetter captures the role of cultural understandings in entrepreneurship for middleman minorities. He recounts Peter Gosling's description of how an ethnic Chinese shopkeeper collects his debts in a Malay village:

> [The Chinese shopkeeper] appeared to be considerably acculturated to Malay culture, and was scrupulously sensitive to Malays in every way, including the normal wearing of sarong, quiet and polite Malay speech, and a humble and affable manner. However, at harvest time when he would go to the field to collect crops

on which he had advanced credit, he would put on his Chinese costume of shorts and undershirt, and speak in a much more abrupt fashion, acting, as one Malay farmer put it, "just like a Chinese." (Gosling quoted in Granovetter 1995: 148)

The Chinese shopkeeper creates a sense of the occasion through his costume and his speech. This sense of the situation constitutes the manner in which some types of monies are to be collected, and without this dramaturgical performance, the debtors might not regard the collection as legitimate or the collector might not come across as being right in insisting that the debt be paid at that particular time.

Ivan Light and Steven Gold (Light and Gold 2000) offer a useful discussion of ethnic enterprises and the importance of social ties and culture for their operations. He shows how ethnic enterprises operate within a *moral community*. Ascriptive ties matter in creating group solidarity. So too does the reception of the broader society. Social solidarity varies by ethnic group (because of culture) and these variations have an impact on economic organization and economic outcomes. Norms of trust emerge as families and family reputation act as collateral against default. Culture remains, however, under-theorized in these accounts.

The expectations and understandings within an ethnic group significantly affect how entrepreneurs obtain capital. For cultural reasons, some ethnic groups are more likely to assist their co-ethnics with capital to start-up businesses. "Young and Sontz ... found that only 24 percent of Hispanic grocers received help from friends or family when starting up, but 57 percent of Korean grocers had received that help" (Light and Karageorgis 1994: 658). Similarly, groups engaged in rotating credit associations have a tradition that facilitates entrepreneurship relative to groups who do not have such a tradition. In this way, social networks help us understand founding conditions for some of these enterprises.

Alejandro Portes and Alex Stepick (1994) identify different definitions of the situation and how values are introjected into members of a bounded community within the Cuban enclave. Instead of thinking about one-on-one dyadic relationships and network ties, Portes theorizes how individuals orient their behaviors to conform to the expectations generally held within their bounded group, where an overarching set of norms governs behavior. In the case of the Cuban enclave, any Cuban who did not repay a loan to the bank knew that he would lose a great deal of status in the community and that he would be shunned socially and made into a pariah. The social sanctions would come from people from outside the bank. Rather than worrying about a one-on-one relationship, the lender has to worry about how the group might view his actions and how the group might respond. Moreover, value introjection means that the individual has internalized norms of altruism toward members of his or her group and feels the force of those norms, even in circumstances where others might not learn about her breaching those norms.

The Culture of Companies

The culture of organizations leads suppliers of goods and services to develop their own understandings about right and wrong. People assume roles, and they understand that with their roles comes a specialized way in which they should see the world. As a result, a person working for NASA can take on the role of "engineer" and decide that the launch of a spacecraft is too risky given the condition of the craft and of the launch apparatus; however, that same person can then assume the role of "manager" and decide that so long as standard operating procedures have been followed, the launch is justified. The cultural beliefs within the organization made cutting corners seem like the right thing to do; so long as these actions did not specifically violate the rules of operation. Seemingly minor exceptions to the rules that seemed to remain within the confines of the standard procedures were tolerated, but as minor modifications piled up, so too did the risk to life and to property. This is the explanation given by sociologist Diane Vaughan (1996) to explain why the Space Shuttle Challenger disaster happened in 1986, not because information about the problem-ridden O-rings was not available, but rather because the culture of organizational life made such concerns banal.

Analogously, within firms people take on roles and they come to understand what the standard operating procedures of the bureaucracy are. Even when these procedures do not facilitate the firm's ultimate goals, they are followed, nonetheless. In *Moral Mazes,* Robert Jackall explains that firms have their own interpretive lenses that make sense of the world, and as individuals operate within these work cultures, they find that their sense of ethics changes. Jackall defines occupational ethics to mean "the moral rules-in-use that managers construct to guide their behavior at work, whether these are shaped directly by authority relationships or by other kinds of experiences typical in big organizations" (Jackall [1988] 2010: 2). The financial disaster that befell the banking sector of the United States in 2008 can be understood through the occupational ethics that enabled people in the financial sector to sow the seeds of their own destruction.

> Investment bankers typically hail from top business schools. There they are drilled in the imperative of increasing the value of the assets in their care in as short a time as possible and by any means necessary, without regard for the overall well-being of their own organizations ... They made and continue to make the market for the bundling and securitization for home mortgages, corporate bonds, and commercial real estate loans. They create ... complex derivative instruments that ... [are] opaque and baffling even to putative experts. The derivatives chain financial institutions to each other in ways that prove fatal when the market declines. (Jackall [1988] 2010: 236)

The Cultural Dimensions of Market Supply

The organizational culture that teaches investment bankers what to see as beneficial and what time frames are appropriate for evaluation enabled them to place their own firms along with the entire US economy in grave danger. In their own minds, they were not breaking the law, acting with malice, or conducting wrongheaded evaluations of their own actions; instead, they were complying with the culture of their firms and the occupational ethics that the culture renders germane.

To understand what these occupational ethics are, one has to get into the mind of the corporation. What are its symbols, what are the phrases that are commonly used and what do these phrases mean? Jackall offers an example of the meanings of what people say, how they are to be decoded, and how the ambiguity of the phrases enables managers to move dexterously within a company.

Stock Phrase	Probable Intended Meaning
Exceptionally well qualified	Has committed no major blunders to date
Tactful in dealing with superiors	Knows when to keep his mouth shut
Quick thinking	Offers plausible excuses
Meticulous attention to detail	A nitpicker
Slightly below average	Stupid
Unusually loyal	Wanted by no one else
Indifferent to instruction	Knows more than one's superior
Strong adherence to principles	Stubborn
Requires work–value attitudinal Re-adjustment	Lazy and hardheaded

(Jackall [1988] 2010: 143)

Managers speak in code, and those people who do not understand the code, who cannot speak the language, are not invited into the circle of management. Managers themselves do not have to translate this language to themselves each time it is uttered; after all, the language is theirs, so too the culture. By virtue of repeating, playing with, and upholding the code, managers show themselves committed to the organizational culture.

Karen Ho's (2009) ethnography of Wall Street describes the frames people use to understand and evaluate what they are doing, the social performances individuals enact to establish their credentials and to convince their clients of the worthiness of an investment, and the ritual interactions that make some of their performances resonate as real (authentic). The bankers tell stories to simplify the history of their industry and of their specific firm and to naturalize what they are doing so that other ways of organizing investment banking and evaluating shareholder value remain outside of their evaluative frames. These stories "authorize" the practices within the firm, making them sensible and germane (Certeau 1984).

Karen Ho "approach[es] Wall Street historiographies of shareholder entitlement and Wall Street's conception of itself as fundraiser to the world as origin myths, indicative of a particular worldview and socioeconomic interest rather than objective statements of fact" (Ho 2009: 29). The work units within the Bankers Trust New York Corporation had both a "back-" and a "front-office." Ho describes the difference in status for each office and the demographic and dramaturgical differences between the performers and the performance spaces in the back versus the front. In the back office people of color and white women comprised the majority population. In terms of functions and roles, Ho notes: "Given the hierarchical structure of investment banks, front-office workers, such as investment bankers, traders, and investment managers who take credit for all profits and deals done, depend on the back office for daily support, all the while looking for ways to restructure these 'cost centers'" (Ho 2009: 16). The moral character of the individuals at the investment firm was linked to their location in the front-versus the back-office: the former, smart, innovative, driven; the latter, dim "nine-to-fivers" lacking drive.

The initiation of a deal relies on the ritual presentation

of "the pitch book" with its spreadsheets, graphs, executive summarizes, and strategic recommendations. The pitch books themselves are ceremonial rather than instrumental tools: "Jason Kedd, an investment banking associate ... declared, 'Yeah, we spend so much time on the pitch books, making them look good; they're full of bullshit. After we win the deal, we just toss 'em'" (Ho 2009: 105).

How do consultants and investment bankers initiate a sales pitch, what types of materials do they carry with them and what do they wear to the sales pitch, how do the clients respond to the pitch, and what are the adjustments the presentation team can anticipate making and what are the follow-up encounters the team can expect to have before having the client accept the pitch, request extensive modifications to the plan, or reject the plan outright? The identities and status of the presentation team and the client influences the scripts they anticipate using and the imagery that will be attached to their actions. The imagery (symbols, myths, costumes) helps to solidify the identity of the presentation team members and of the client as both take positions and engage in interaction. Re-definitions of the situation and of the players emerge from the interaction. Some of the actors become fictive kin (Ho 2009: 13), bound by unspoken understandings informally enforced by members of the group as well as third-party actors in the audience.

Likewise, individuals engaged in futures trading are nested within the imagery (collective representations) of sport and battle. Peter Levin examines futures trading and how these dominant metaphors enable individuals to give an account for the what, why, and how of their actions on the trading floor. A twenty-four year-old male pit clerk recalls how he handles the stress of failure: "It's like when you make an error when you're playing baseball. I played sports my whole life, and whenever you made an error, you sat there and moped about it, chances were the next time ... the ball was hit to you, you're going to make an error again. So you, it's like ... just forget about it.

And how weird is that, that you say to yourself, OK, forget about the fact that I just lost $12,000 for that guy, let's go back to work. That's challenging" (Levin 2001: 121). These collective representations of what competition is and how it works include some people but not others. Men can more easily see other men as appropriate participants in a baseball game, but they need not think about women as real players. Extending the metaphor further than Levin, I would describe the split as a binary one between the hard (baseball) and the soft (softball), the center (male) and the periphery (female).

Levin identifies two evaluative frames evident on the trading floor: that of competence and that of sexualized difference. These frames help to spur the workers to be more productive than they might have been otherwise, and to justify why the conditions of work (whether they be dangerous or interesting) are appropriate for a particular class of people. The competence frame obscured the gendered logics working through it. While "competence" is available to anyone who can "get the job done," and therefore does not explicitly rely on gendered logics, competence also requires that the individual "handle stress" in a way the group deems appropriate and that the individual be both aggressive and physically vigorous in getting the job done (Levin 2001: 120).

Yelling and being physical constitute the social performance of futures trading. Just as an actor might employ a voice coach, "some traders go to voice therapists to strengthen their voices to be heard" in the trading pits (Levin 2001: 123). While on the trading floor, the traders recognize that the space is tightly blocked (in the dramaturgical sense) with bodies pressing from the front, the sides, and behind. How the stage is blocked affects who feels most comfortable playing a role with such uncomfortable physical requirements. Similarly, jokes constitute a meta-performance where some men may dominate with enactments of bawdy, juvenile, sexual behavior – leaving the women to retreat or to stand at the margins of the meta-performance in order to demonstrate that they have "thick skins" and are not too sensitive (weak). After an altercation between two clerks, they used highly sexualized language to diffuse the tension with a joke: "[O]ne said to the other, 'You weigh 100 pounds more than me, you could probably beat up my sister too.' The second clerk's response, *both to the clerk and laughing onlookers*, was 'Yeah, I could, but I'd fuck her first. Up the ass!'" [emphasis added] (Levin 2001: 124). The jokes clearly are not told for the sake of a single individual but are directed toward an audience of onlookers, as individuals compete for dominance in attention space. In the course of the performance, group solidarities manifest themselves along with status hierarchies within and between groups (Collins 2004).

Whether the frame of competence or the frame of sexualized difference is activated depends on the more fluid moments of day ("lunch hours, coffee breaks, speedups, slowdowns" (Levin 2001: 127) as well as the temporally rigid opening and closing bells. Correlated with these frames are scripts, ordering action, inserting conquest- and joke-telling periods, having one's voice be heard (or not) as the attractive female runner enters and exits the trading floor. These sequenced actions differ by gender of the performer and his or her status position within the pit. One might imagine that a lower-status individual within the pit may manifest his or her status ascent by engaging in a different script (one utilized by a higher status individual). As individuals seek respect and deference in their places of work, they may have to do more than simply earn more money or demonstrate more competence. They may also have to adopt scripts that bolster their accomplishments in order for their achievements to resonate as real for the relevant audiences.

Trading floors are performance spaces where the actors perform on the pit's stage (Abolafia 1996; Zaloom 2006) or literally on screen (Knorr-Cetina and Bruegger 2002; Preda 2008). There are scopes (collective representations and frames) that facilitate how actors evaluate and act within the electronic trading world. A scope, or scopic system, is "an instrument for seeing or observing ... an arrangement of hardware, software, and human feeds that together function like a scope: like a mechanisms of observation and projection, here collecting, augmenting, and transmitting the reality of the markets, their internal environments and external context" (Knorr-Cetina 2009: 64).

Knorr-Cetina has begun to develop a Goffmanian approach to analyze electronic transactions and foreign exchange markets. Three assumptions of the Goffmanian situation have to be relaxed or disregarded so that Knorr-Cetina can develop her concept of the synthetic situation:

- The assumption that the prototypical unit of an interaction order is a physical setting and involves the physical co-presence of participants.
- The assumption that the interaction order can be based theoretically on territorial relatedness rather than on the temporalities of encounters.
- The assumption that there is somehow a deep divide between the interaction order and the situational dynamics at the core of microanalysis, and structure or macrosocial phenomena. (Knorr-Cetina 2009: 63)

How does transferring electronic media help to establish or bolster categorical identities within electronic exchange situations? What are the mechanisms for third-party enforcement?

Rather than bodily co-presence, Khorr-Cetina writes of the *response presence* – "the interacting party is not or need not be physically present but is accountable for responding without inappropriate delay to an incoming attention or interaction request" (Knorr-Cetina 2009: 74). The response presence enables actors to coordinate and sustain their actions. In the case of electronic trading, the actors must practice preparedness, being ready "to respond to trading challenges that appear on-screen" (74) and these challenges will be sequenced and expressed in specialized language: the language itself marking insiders from outsiders; the pace of the interchange indicating the transaction's intensity.

1 FROM GB6 [Name of Bank]INTL LONDON * 1301GMT 251196*/3514
2 Our terminal: GB1Z Our user:[Name of Spot Dealer]
3 # TEST BACK LOWER RATES NOW …
4 #
5 #INTERRUPT#
6 CAN I GIVE YOU 15 MIO USDCHF PLS
7 # SURE 83
8 GTEATEE TREE GREAT. TKS
9 # WELCOME…
10 # BUYING DM SFR HERE…
11 # AROUND 150 MI…
12 # BUT LOOKS DAMN TOPPISH HERE … THINKING [GB4]… ON THE TOP
14 # … (Knorr-Cetina 2009: 75)

This synthetic situation between traders in Zurich and London trading dollars for Swiss francs illustrates the actor's preparedness to deal with the decline in the dollar's value and the courtesies extended as they negotiate the deal. Indeed, a process of matching does take place. Currencies are treated as if they have "moods"; so an anxious and volatile currency like the Italian lira was often matched with a trader deemed to be moody (Knorr-Cetina 2009: 78). The emotional energy of the interaction sustains the actors who have embodied the (gut) instincts for dealing with particular types of information (Collins 2004).

The Power of Categories

Definitional categories are consequential for how companies perform in the stock market and for how individuals perform in the labor market. This section begins with how we categorize things and why these categories have economic consequences for market suppliers. The section concludes with how we categorize people, relying on understandings about racial identities and cultural lifestyles to help us in sorting quality and qualities in the labor market. To these two modes of categorization we now turn.

Categories of Things

Ezra Zuckerman demonstrates how meanings guide action in the American Stock Exchange. Examining stock prices between 1985 and 1994, Zuckerman contrasts a non-cultural perspective (which cannot account for the changes in price) versus a cultural one (which can). In the non-cultural version of market analysis, buyers engage in "rational choice among legitimate alternatives" (Zuckerman 1999: 1404), but in a cultural analysis, these "rational" choices happen in the second, rather than the first, instance.

> Consumers first screen out illegitimate options, and only then do they perform something akin to rational choice among legitimate alternatives. Second, the screen is a social screen, not designed by the actor but external to her, given in the categories that comprise market structure. Products that deviate from accepted categories are penalized not simply because they raise information costs for consumers but because the social boundaries that divide product classes limit the consideration of such offerings.

In the cultural version, each market actor understands her own actions and the actions of others in relation to the roles each is understood to enact. Likewise, an object, whether it be a product, a characteristic of a good or a service, or a price, is understandable to the extent that it can be compared with existing categories. Anything new must conform somehow to the old to be recognizable, for without reference to existing categories, individual actors do not know what to do with the new. This leads to the generation of narratives about what things are and how they "fit" into existing understandings (Zuckerman 1999: 1398–9). These narratives are not an epiphenomenon of material struggle but co-constitutive of such struggles. The narratives and the categorical understandings they represent guide action in the marketplace with verifiable consequences.

Zuckerman marshals evidence of the negative consequences that ensue from defying or falling outside of prevailing interpretive frameworks (categories). Organizational case studies and theoretical syntheses had pointed to conformity as evidence that there are patterned actions and forms across a diverse set of organizations; however, these studies had not shown diverse outcomes. Sampling on the dependent variable, the case studies described situations of conformity and then noted how a prevailing interpretive frame made it inevitable. Were there cases of nonconformity, and if so, why did the prevailing interpretive frame not correct it?

Nearly taking a Goffmanian turn, Zuckerman addresses the audiences that confer legitimacy on an actor's performance and on objects of interest. Although Zuckerman does not use the Goffmanian language of performance, the same metaphors apply. The actors on stage should seem to believe in the parts that they are playing. When the actor begins to fall out of her role by dropping an expected line or fumbling a prop, the actor attempts to cover the mistake with tact. So long as the actors are respecting the audience's prevailing understanding about what kind of performance is being enacted, the audience will respond with tact, regarding the tact the performers themselves have shown. If the actors seem to disrespect these prevailing understandings, the performance falls flat. Zuckerman

The Cultural Dimensions of Market Supply

(1999: 1401, *comments in italics not in original*) describes this dynamic as the candidate-audience interface:

> Consider a very simple social situation: an interface between two classes of actors [...] the first set of actors, whom I term "candidates," seeks entry into relations with members of the second class, whom I call "the audience." Candidates present the audience with different "offers" in an attempt to win their favor ... The latter seek to assess the relative worth of the offers presented by the former [*who seem to believe in the parts they are playing*]. However, evaluation requires calibration of offers against one another. Offers that do not exhibit certain common characteristics may not be readily compared to others and are thus difficult to evaluate [*the performance goes off track, lines are dropped, props fumbled, inappropriate ad-libbing*]. Such offers stand outside the field of comparison and are ignored as so many oranges in a competition among apples [*performance falls flat*]. It is this inattention that constitutes the cost of illegitimacy.

The audience response is critical for the actors whose performance is being observed. Applause (purchases) can be loud (high price) or muted (low price). In the worse case scenario, there is no applause (no purchases). Subtle reactions from the audience help the actors understand how well their performance is being taken. Because of the dynamics in the candidate-audience interface, most innovations fail. The audience does not expect the next line; the blocking of each scene seems "unnatural" for the narrative. The innovation simply does not make sense, so the audience does not "buy" (believe in) the performance (as legitimate).

In Zuckerman's study, the critics who evaluate market securities constitute the audience. These critics specialize in product categories and evaluate the quality of the securities being traded. When there is a strong match between the analyst's area of expertise and the object's conformity to the existing product category, the price of the security is considered legitimate.

However, when there is a mismatch because the object falls outside of existing categories, the security suffers from an illegitimacy discount, and its price declines.

Likewise, Zuckerman and his colleagues examine what happens when there is a mismatch between an actor's categorical genre and the parts that the actor wishes to play in the movies. Their data come from the Internet Movie Database (IMDB) from 1992–4 and they ask what how hard is it for an actor to move from one genre to another in the time-period of 1995 to 1997 after having established an identity within a particular genre during the earlier time-period. For those actors who manage to continue getting work, they are most likely to remain in the same genre. The actor's identity enters into the actor-audience interface facilitating employment for some genres while restricting it for others. When a movie actor is typecast, her identity becomes less ambiguous and easier to imagine as believable for general audiences. As one talent agent put it, "[I]n show business, most actors and actresses only get 15 minutes of fame. Being typecast is a way... to extend those 15 minutes into a possible career. I'd swear by typecasting, especially just starting out. Typecasting can be just like a foot-in-the-door. It's great to be known and consistently hired" (Zuckerman, Kim, Ukanwa, and Rittmann 2003: 1039).

Although typecasting opens up doors for specific types of roles, it precludes the actor's suitability for other roles. One actress explained, "Because I am a large, black woman ... I will always play someone's other, someone poor, the neighbor. Shakespeare? Yeah, right. Next" (Zuckerman et al. 2003: 1040)! The casting directors interviewed in the study recognized this dynamic and the disadvantages it carries, but they seemed to feel that it would be difficult to alter the state of affairs:

> It's hard all the time to, you know, be open-minded about everything. I think we're all *guilty* of, you know, playing the typecasting

part, for sure ... It's an advantage on one side of it just because ... timing-wise it just helps to know that there's people out there that can fit certain characteristics. And you know on the other side, the disadvantage is you're not giving the people that are typecast a chance to try something different. (It's) not necessarily (a disadvantage to me though). It's a disadvantage to the actors [italics added]. (Zuckerman et al. 2003: 1040)

These identity constraints result from minimizing risk and typecasting from attenuating information asymmetries. Categories of work and categories of persons are imperfectly matched, and what happens in the opening scene of the matching process (to use the language of dramaturgy) affects what may happen in the subsequent scenes.

Categories of Persons

Now let's imagine how the evaluations of teachers, trainers, employers, and colleagues draws on collective narratives about race, leisure, and moral worth. It would be a mistake to look for outright racism in corporate cultures. Perhaps the term racist is too loaded to help with the analytics of how jobs and favorable evaluations get distributed to differently categorized persons. This section will look at working-class men in a vocational school, corporate executives, and new professional entrants to the financial sector to see how culture shapes the opportunities for these people in their respective labor markets.

Deirdre Royster's study of fifty working-class men at the Glendale Vocational High School illustrates how cultural understandings about race and ethnicity affect how people experience labor markets. Often people who study culture in markets leave race aside. This is partly due to the traditional emphasis on racial animus (prejudicial attitudes, ethnic hatred) as a source of labor market discrimination; however, Royster's study demonstrates how a coded language about race, how the types of music that people listen to or are presumed to

75

listen to, and how other styles of life enter into calculations about who makes a good apprentice and who should get extra opportunities to gain work experience.

Royster interviews equal numbers of black and white men in the same vocational training program and tries to explain why the white students from the program have fared better than the black ones in getting matched with employers after school, holding training and grades earned in school constant. She found that background representations of how the labor market works and who the "real" competitors are in it play a significant role in limiting the parts that people may play. A number of stories circulate among job seekers and potential employers and these stories provide interpretive lenses (frames) for understanding why some people do or do not get matched to their job of choice. The mythical hardships encountered by whites experiencing "reverse discrimination" (a widely circulated narrative) functions as a frame for interpreting a job seeker's worth and how to evaluate a match or a failure to match. For example, a state police applicant (who is white) was not selected for a follow-up interview and interpreted it through the frame of reverse discrimination: "I applied for the state police and I passed all the tests and stuff like that. And we were down there for something. I forget what it was. And one of the [white] state troopers (we were on the side – a group of white male individuals), he said to us – [because] we obviously weren't selected to go further in pre-employment – he said, 'I'm sorry fellas. Unfortunately, if you were black you would have had the job'" (Royster 2003: 4). He offers a justification for why his own behavior is done for the sake of justice. Rather than denying work for an African-American, he sees himself as helping a group of people who are being denied opportunities to compete fairly. He uses the same trope of justice and fairness as anyone else would in a free-market society.

These notions of justice have significant effects on which

students get matched with which employers at the end of their vocational program. By a student's third year, he usually has entered (or tried to enter) the work–study program, meant to facilitate employee–employer matches. The students operate within circuits circumscribed by race, and these circuits lead them into either formal or informal work–study programs, with the latter often more lucrative. As Royster follows the paths taken by black and white students, she finds that their white, male instructors use different media in their white circuits compared with their black circuits of students. I use the term media loosely to note the favors, advice, equipment, letters of recommendation, work contracts, or other material or non-material items transferred from one party to another. Each actor uses different baskets of transaction media for differently defined actors, yet it is all done in the name of fairness and seen by the teachers as fair.

Compare these two students who learned from and admired the same teacher, Mr Spano. The black student "listed Mr Spano as someone who had offered to write letters of recommendation, make phone calls, or serve as a reference if necessary," but the black student did not use Mr Spano's name as a reference because he did not *sense* that doing so would be helpful. Royster probed to find out more about the dynamics of Mr Spano's offer to help the black student: "*He extended his hand to, like, put in a word for you, but you didn't follow up on that job, or...*" [emphasis in the original]? The young man replied, "He never really set up no jobs or nothing like that but he said if he knew somebody that needed some people he would recommend me" (Royster 2003: 120). By contrast, a white student she interviewed recalled more warmth and outreach from the same Mr Spano:

> Spano – he was more of a friend to everybody than a teacher, he'd help us with other teachers, like if we got into trouble, he'd go find out what was the trouble.

The Cultural Dimensions of Market Supply

I: Did any of your instructors offer to write letters for you...

Yes, they would. He'd [Spano] find us jobs, whatever we wanted. If we were willing to find jobs, he'd find us a place to work, if we wanted work.

I: Did you get a job as a result of this kind of help?

Yes, the tile job, and then he gave me a lot of side jobs. (Royster 2003: 121)

Royster suggests that the teachers did not consciously place black students at a disadvantage and that the teachers encouraged and had good relations with their black students; however, when the time came for action, the teachers took for granted the types of transfers they made toward white students compared with those made toward black students. Perhaps these teachers were responding to their own perception that the black students would not need as much help in an environment where affirmative action would take care of their employment needs. The teachers certainly responded to what they saw as "overreactions" and to a musical taste for rap as behavioral (dramaturgical) indications that a particular student would not "fit" well into the teacher's circuit of mentees. These evaluations (frames) correlate to specific sequences of action. In some cases, not only did the teacher talk about job opportunities and offer to write letters of reference, but they also looked for available jobs on behalf of their students, let their students use the teacher's personal tools, and hired the students for side jobs so that the students could get more hands-on experience for the job market. In other words, collective stories about how fairness and opportunity are distributed and about the lifestyles of the rap-adoring African-American students played a significant role in what opportunities they would find in the labor market.

Likewise, Elijah Anderson notes that African-American professionals find themselves operating with what Erving Goffman calls a "spoiled identity." Using Goffman's discussion of stigma,

78

Anderson notes that African-Americans are marked by their skin-color, so they cannot cover their stigmata and pretend to be like everyone else. Instead, they must manage their stigma. One of the Black corporate executives that Anderson interviewed described the leisure activities of the Black colleagues in his social circle and how these activities affected how their White colleagues received them in the firm:

> In terms of their lifestyles, some do the opera thing and the art museum thing. But all black executives will also do the jazz. They also do the house party. They wouldn't do it with the core group, but it would be a high-class house party ... You'd have two different sets of agendas: one where you'd want to create some cohesion with some of the whites so they could see how nice you could socialize, but where you'd really want to let yourself go and get down and talk about issues, then it would be blacks only ... About ten, twelve years ago, my wife bought me some golf clubs for Christmas. I never thought about playing golf before that. She said, You need these to be part of the team. So I took up golf. (quoted in Anderson 1999: 13–14)

These executives understand that what types of games one plays, being able to pick up a tennis racket, and having close interactions with colleagues by virtue of playing on a team together influence how these executives will be regarded and what types of opportunities will lie ahead for them in the company.

Lauren Rivera (2011), a sociologist who teaches at the Kellogg School of Business (Northwestern), finds that leisure activities are seen as a marker of moral character by employers. Football and basketball are the rough; lacrosse and crew, the refined. Job applicants landing a lucrative position on Wall Street are more likely to come from the refined than from the rough. Rivera does not dwell on the racial implications of these categories, but one can see that racial and ethnic minorities do not find themselves on the crew team with the same likelihood as on the basketball team. Cultural understandings about race and leisure help structure who gets a job, all other things being equal.

Conclusion

This chapter has outlined the cultural dimensions of market supply. The rationale of how companies operate are culturally inflected and ritually inscribed. From one social setting or one time-period to the next, there are variations in what seems logical and different approaches to how production and distribution should be executed. As we dig into the historical and the ethnographic detail of production, the fictions of pure rationality fall away. Companies and entire industries are animated by charismatic personalities, concerns for justice, coded language, and dramaturgically playful contests. To miss these is to misunderstand how and why market suppliers do what they do.

3

The Culture of Money and Prices

Most people have been told that money is money, so a person's gender, social class, ethnicity, caste, or tribe matters not. So long as she can pay, she can play in the marketplace. This chapter challenges these common sensical understandings of what money is and what it does. Re-thinking money (and the transactions in which we use it) is not merely an academic exercise, relevant only to theorists or to people deeply engaged in narrow studies of economic life. Such a re-think enables us to understand situations that standard accounts of money and markets do not.

The countries of Western Europe decide that creating a single currency (the euro) will facilitate trade across their borders and promote economic growth for their region. The creation of a currency should be a technical problem more than a political one, yet there were great difficulties over its implementation as the countries participating in the single currency discussed what the currency would look like. What symbols would adorn it and what would these symbols mean? Some country leaders expressed concern that the European Union would fail to create a single currency due to symbolic, rather than financial, concerns. Why do the images on the money matter so much, if money is just money?

Modern art galleries sometimes find that an artist has one set of paintings selling well but another set selling poorly. Clearly the market is sending a message that one set is more highly valued by buyers than the other set, so the gallery should reduce the price on the paintings selling poorly. This pricing logic, however, does not hold for modern art galleries where they refuse to price same-sized art by the same artists according to how well it sells. How does money work in these art markets? What does this tell us about the cultural constraints on how money moves in different market contexts?

For a long time, economists thought that households have a single budget, and that whatever money comes into the household adds up to the household's total budget; however, the way that these households were spending their money made little sense. Instead of realizing that they had a single budget constraint from which to operate, these households acted as if the wife's money had to go toward groceries and school supplies, the husband's toward rent, and the children's toward school supplies and recreation. Why couldn't they act as one, making more strategic decisions about budgeting? Why does the identity of who earned the money (or how it was obtained) matter for how the money is spent?

This chapter will walk through these three examples to show how money works at the national/international level, how it works in specific industries, and how it works within households. At each level of analysis, we are forced to reformulate what we mean by money and to open our minds to the many functions that money and prices serve. It is not simply a means for engaging in market exchange; it is also a carrier of meanings and a useful prop for use in rituals and in other public performances. After reviewing national, market, and household monies, we will examine how money gets used in to engage in what Viviana Zelizer calls relational work – the use of money and other exchange media to affirm, contest, or dissolve the meanings of the relationships that people believe themselves to be in. In other words, the way one uses money and gifts in an intimate relationship differs from the way one uses it for casual acquaintances or for one-shot (sometimes one-night) encounters. These examples can be extended into the business world, and when we arrive at this section toward the end of this chapter, we'll do just that. Before turning to the three examples of national, market, and household monies, let's first explain what we mean by money.

What is money?

We often think of money as legal tender (dollar bills, for example), but it takes a number of different forms. Tokens, cigarettes, frequent flier points, and loyalty credits have also stood in as money, facilitating exchange. And even within the framework of legal tender, sometimes a dollar gets marked, earmarked, or ritually transformed into a different kind of money. By different monies, I mean we take a bit of cash and call it a name. The name might be "grocery money," "gas money," "newspaper delivery money," or something else. The physical paper has not changed, but the way we use it and the restrictions we place on it have.

This view of multiple monies treats paper money like any other object that gets socially marked for specific purposes. Money has taken the forms of copper bracelets (manillas), sea-shells (zimbos and cowries), coral, dried fish, furs, nails, and cotton cloth. In fact, in Monomotapa at the Gulf of Guinea, cotton cloth served as the local currency used to purchase male slaves. In time, the large piece of cloth became known as "a piece of India" (designating its size as being in no way small) became a common expression for a male slave (Braudel 1981: 442). The language of money originated from local practices and shared understandings about how things should be exchanged.

Viviana Zelizer (2001: 991) describes money as having the following three properties: (1) it facilitates the transfer of the rights to a good or serve; (2) it may be used generally in a variety of sites and among a diverse set of individuals; and (3) it stores mutually recognized economic value. The more an object is made to satisfy these criteria, the more money-like it is. Legal tender, therefore, is money *par excellence*.

In the modern economy, some theorists regarded these old conceptions of money as obsolete, whether or not these other forms of money satisfied the three criteria outlined by Zelizer. Money came to represent a quantified token of value, backed up by a trustworthy central bank. Money had moved from being a plurality of objects and currencies to being a single format within a national territory; however, the way that people have treated their money has meant that it cannot be used as if it does not have particular or different meanings as it moves from one transaction context to the next.

In some pre-modern societies, cattle served the functions of money, but this type of money served several functions, enabling market exchange and marking the types of relationships that people were in. For example, anthropologist Evans-Pritchard describes how cattle transfers mark relationships among the Nuer people while also acting as a medium of exchange.

> The network of kinship ties which links members of local communities is brought about by the operation of exogamous rules, *often stated in terms of cattle. The union of marriage is brought about by the payment of cattle and every phase of the ritual is marked by their transference or slaughter.* The legal status of the partners is defined by cattle rights and obligations.

> Cattle are owned by families ... As each son, in order of seniority, reaches the age of marriage he marries with cows from the herd ... *Kinship is customarily defined by reference to these payments*, being most clearly pointed at marriage, when movements of cattle from kraal to kraal are equivalent to lines in a genealogical chart ... Nuer tend to define all social processes and relationships in terms of cattle. Their social idiom is a bovine idiom. [emphasis added] (Evans-Pritchard in Douglas and Isherwood 1979: 39)

One need only see from whom the cattle flow and in what way to know that the donor is the father and the recipient his first versus his second son or that the occasion is marriage. To know who does not receive cattle is to know something about the category of relationship the individual does not have with the donor. The language of society is the language of money (or some other exchange medium).

Analogously, in modern societies people establish what their relationships are by virtue of the relative amount and the directional flow of their exchange media. Who gives and who receives what media (be it cattle, cash, or tokens)? What is the style of the transfer? What are the debates (the narratives) that praise or protest the amount, the direction, and/or the style of the transaction? These narratives and flows enable us to pin down the cultural meanings that guide transactions in the marketplace and to understand the types, meanings, and functions of money.

National Monies

Perhaps Emily Gilbert and Eric Helleiner said it best: "If money served only an economic purpose, it is unlikely that it would have been traditionally organized largely along national lines … National currencies, and money more generally, need to be examined not just as an economic phenomenon but also in terms of their geographic, political, social and cultural dynamics" (Gilbert and Helleiner 1999: 1–2). These dynamics present themselves during transitions that threaten the cultural meanings of currencies. This makes the case of the euro an excellent one for seeing how populations, that had long taken for granted the meanings of money, awaken to protect the symbols and national meanings imbued in their currency (Dodd 1994). One side of the euro is symbolically neutral while the other side is marked with a national symbol of a particular member country.

These attentions to symbolic detail allowed people to feel that the supranational currency remained somehow national. In his introduction to *The Year of the Euro* (2006), Robert Fishman depicts just how charged the changeover was in 2002.

> The scenes of euro enthusiasts lining up beside automatic teller machines to withdraw new euro banknotes shortly after midnight on the changeover date, the confusion and petty disputes over currency conversion in some commercial establishments, and indeed all the many stories and experiences constituting the year of the euro stand as an enormous collective … experience spanning twelve European countries. (Fishman 2006: 8)

In the same volume Jacques Hymans writes of the importance of the new currency for forging a sense of a shared European Union identity, and he points to the "iconography… the values, themes, and concepts represented by artistic motifs [on the money]… [as assisting] in the construction of a European identity" (Hymans 2006: 15). Hymans carefully notes that state governments did not impose cultural symbols on their populations but rather accepted the symbols already resonant with their respective populations: "In other words, far from trying to use their control of currency to impose statist values on a recalcitrant citizenry, states are more likely to try to increase their legitimacy by using the currency to signal their embrace of values in tune with the 'spirit of the times'" (Hymans 2004: 6).

Analogously, in the United States, the national currency was also seen as an important vehicle for forging national identity. Eric Helleiner uses an 1863 letter from the S. M. Clark, the chief clerk of the US Treasury, addressed to Secretary Salmon Chase, in order to illustrate how the producers of currency intend to disseminate nationalist images through the circulation of money in the marketplace. The letter reads:

> [The money] would tend to teach the masses the prominent periods in our nation's history. The laboring man who should receive every

The Culture of Money and Prices

Saturday night, a copy of "Surrender of Burgoyne" for his weekly wages, would soon inquire who General Burgoyne was, and to whom he surrendered. This curiosity would be aroused and he would learn the facts from a fellow laborer or from his employer. The same would be true of other National pictures, and in time many would be taught leading incidents in our country's history, so that they would soon be familiar to those who would never read them in books, teaching them history and imbuing them with a National feeling. (Helleiner 1998: 1412)

Because money is widely circulated voluntarily by people who happen to use the market for procuring their needs, the state does not have to force a sense of national feeling. The national culture would cohere by virtue of consumption and economic exchange. As individuals engage in their routines and move through their daily rounds, they encounter monies and the images carried thereon.

Bruce Carruthers and Sarah Babb (1996) explain the debates over the national currency in the United States after the Civil War. At the time, there were different forms of money that needed to be unified so that the national government could pay its war debts. The forms of money included "national bank notes, state bank notes, greenbacks, currency convertible into specie, and specie coin" (Carruthers and Babb 1996: 1557). There were two schools of thought about what form the national currency should take. The bullionists (advocates of "hard money") challenged the greenbackers (advocates of "soft money"). For the former, money had an intrinsic value and its holders were honest Christians (not pagan shape shifters); therefore, the currency should be made out of a material that could itself be bought and sold in its own right. For the latter, money was a democratic creation subject to democratic control, a promise made and kept, guaranteed by a trustworthy government.

Carruthers and Babb demonstrate that the value imbued in gold could have been imbued in paper money, bits of metal, nails, seashells, strips of leather, or any other object. The value of an object is a collective decision and depends on a shared, even if contested, understanding of what ought to serve as money and what symbols most appropriately mark it. To think that a national currency is merely a technical accomplishment is to miss its history and its current operations in the marketplace.

A recent example of market money creation drives the point home. When the government creates new monies, such as "loyalty benefits" or other forms of social insurance, it takes great care to distinguish these transfer payments with distinct names so that the individual receiving those payments understands their relationship with the nation-state. In Israel the government pays loyalty benefits to its citizens who have contributed to civil society by serving in the military or by helping the state bolster its population through immigrating and settling in the Jewish state as a Jew. Other cash benefits are also paid at the completion of compulsory national service and as replacement income for citizens serving in the reserves (Shalev 2009). These transfer payments, the way they are marked with distinctive names, and the bundle of other exchange media transferred to different individuals mark the category of person and the category of the individual's relationship to the nation-state. Through exchange media, the Israeli state works to constitute a collective identity, and it names its currencies carefully.

Market Monies and Prices

Within national borders, there are a number of local markets that create their own rules about how currencies should be used or create new currencies altogether. At the beginning of the chapter, we encountered an art market where the logic of money defied expectation. This section on market monies will begin by examining the case and then will look at how money and prices work in different types of auctions, in local exchange trading systems, and in the stock exchange. This variety of market monies reinforces the notion that there is culture spread across a variety of markets. While art markets seem to be the obvious starting point for looking at cultural logics in money and pricing, one need only re-cast the familiar as strange to see the various normative principles, the dramaturgical acts, and the shared stories that animate and drive market action. Now we turn to art prices.

Sociologist Olav Velthuis studied modern art galleries in both New York and Amsterdam. The shared meanings within the art community led gallery owners to diminish the importance of price by keeping the same-sized artwork from the same artist priced the same, regardless of what the demand was for the different pieces.

> An American dealer explained forcefully: "You cannot price works differently. During the artist's lifetime, whatever you exhibit has to be described as of equal merit. Everything an artist shows is of equal merit." … Dealers who abstain from applying this norm are fully aware of this and are ready to provide a legitimization for their deviating behavior. (Velthuis 2003: 192)

And art dealers established the prices for which to sell art in a way that recognized the artist's place within a community of artist rather than as a way of predicting how much buyers might be willing to spend on a particular artist or on a particular piece.

Just as currencies can help to keep a national identity together, money (prices) kept intact the boundaries of an art community. Art dealers talk about money with their clients in order to take on the role of confidante. The clients have to feel that spending a great deal of money on art is a good idea, and they look to the dealers as informal therapists and friends. At the same time, the dealers use money and prices as a way to draw near to the artists, promoting their self-esteem, and giving them a sense of belonging to a community.

The Culture of Money and Prices

[The dealers take on a caring role toward artists.] Especially young artists who have high expectations and whose self-confidence has grown once they find a gallery ... Dealers [feel that] it is their duty to "protect" these artists against themselves and against the market. Instead of granting those artists the sweet pleasure of high prices, an art dealer can provide them other sources of self-esteem, such as taking their work to art fairs, or achieving critical attention from museums and critics ... This caring role of dealers vis-à-vis artists provides an additional reason to avoid price decreases: they negatively affect the self-esteem of the artists. (Velthuis 2003: 199)

Through pricing strategies, dealers enact their emotional commitments to the artists in their orbit. Money and pricing strategies become a means to generate an economic livelihood while cementing meaningful relationships within a circuit of artists, dealers, and clients.

Charles Smith also examines why prices do not show up as expected in a variety of auction sites. Money and prices become dramaturgical props as individuals come together to enact scripts about fairness and justice. The actors arrive to the metaphorical stage in costume, following "established rituals of dress and behavior as well as the sense of tradition that pervades these auctions" (Smith 1989: 10). Smith writes: "At a thoroughbred horse auction... one is immediately struck by the style of dress of the participants. Although there are a number of exceptions, the standard Lexington attire for men is khaki pants; a solid color, preferably blue, sport or polo, and loafers. Most women dress equivalently in blouse and skirt or pants" (67). From one situation to the next, the uniformity of dress among different types of buyers, different types of sellers, or both help participants to understand what performances are likely to be enacted. From one situation to the next, "[e]veryone knows – even if only tacitly – what is expected and the roles of the various participants. In most department stores, we can tell who are the customers and who are the salespeople, what is a dressing room and what a storage room and what we are to do if we buy a particular item" (Smith 1989: 52). The sequenced actions actors expect to follow also differ in differently defined situations.

During the course of the auction, the prices for goods are established collectively. The money people are willing to pay for the various goods depends on a set of community norms, and the auction leader directs the performance so that the various actors handle money and prices in a culturally appropriate way. Consider Smith's descriptions of two different auctions at Luther's Commodity Auction Barn.

> Though their style is similar, Luther's horse auctions differ considerably from his normal Tuesday auction, which features eggs, chickens, ducks, rabbits, and in the evening, sheep and cattle. Tuesday auctions aim more at a relatively small number of professional buyers hoping to obtain merchandise for their own business. Those in attendance tend to be auction regulars who know each other and constitute a community not unlike that found at the less-select thoroughbred auctions. Los's horse auctions, however, draw a much more heterogeneous group of neighbors and strangers. This explains in part Los's use of humor and stories. For his auctions to be successful, both buyers and sellers must feel that the prices established reflect the views of the community. For this to be true, there must *be* a community of some sort. Creating this community, even if only for a few hours, is perhaps Los's major job. (Smith 1989: 11)

When the views of the community are not reflected in the price or in the sequenced action leading to a purchase, the participants negatively sanction those who violate the script. Other auction participants might inform the violators that they are engaging in "suicidal" behavior. The other participants may also ridicule the violators with gossip or may choose to take it out on them outside of the auction, in those cases where the violator shares financial, work, family, or friendship ties (e.g. Smith 1989: 35).

What happens in the modern art gallery studied by Olav Velthuis and in the auctions examined by Charles Smith is merely an extension of what happens in local exchange trading systems, also known as LETS. Some local people created their own currencies because they feared that legal tender would lead to anonymity and a meaningless social existence. In the community of Newbury, the LETS administrator described the function of the currency as creating a "mental village" (Lang 1994: 32). Unlike the capitalist marketplace where the wealthy can participate more actively than can the poor, the educated more astutely than the uneducated, the LETS marketplace is believed to create a level playing field so that a person's background does not preclude actively buying and selling.

LETS mix legal tender with local currencies so that an individual's purchase can be highly differentiated. Take the example of a LETS participant whose grandniece is planning a trip to China for six months. The budget for the trip relies on local currency (Caring Relationship Tickets), frequent flier points (another form of special monies), and pound sterling (legal tender).

> * Airline travel: paid in frequent-flyer miles that both she and her parents have accumulated.
>
> * Local expenses: she has been saving her "Caring Relationship Tickets" over the past few years by taking care of two elderly neighbors in the university town where she studies. She will simply transfer her credits over the Net to be exchanged for the local currency of the Chinese university town where she plans to live.
>
> * As your Christmas gift, you have decided to add £500 in conventional national currency for incidental expenses that she may have along the way, and as a safety net for any unexpected emergency needs. (Lietaer 2001: 28)

The LETS communities have established reciprocal agreements with each other, and these transactions change the way that the trip itself is valued by the purchasers (the grand-parents, the parents, and the young lady herself). Even the legal tender the grandniece will use on the trip has meaning as it comes not from an anonymous account but rather as a gift given on an annual, socially significant holiday.

Other local currency exchange systems have emerged in reaction to market crises. Because these local currencies were accepted as payment at such global capitalists companies as McDonald's, it demonstrates that there is no clear division between the "regular" market economy where legal tender rules and special markets, these other currencies can circulate outside of tightly bounded communities. A 2001 *New York Times* article reported that about $400 million in goods and services was traded using "scrips" rather than the country's official currency in the year 2000 (Krauss 2001). These alternative currencies were put into circulation by local clubs, but other types of currency were produced and put into circulation by provincial governments. Take, for example, the patacon: "Some businesses here, like McDonald's, have cautiously embraced the new currency. On Wednesday, the chain put up signs announcing 'I believe in my country: I accept patacones' at its restaurants here and began offering a special 'Patacombo,' consisting of two cheeseburgers, medium fries and soft drink, for five patacones – but only if the customer has exact change" (Rohter 2001).

It would be a mistake to think that cultural understandings of monies and transactions only matter for "special" market situations and anomalies. It also matters for what happens at the stock exchange. In Caitlin Zaloom's *Out of the Pits*, we find traders accounting for their gains and losses in the trading pit by using different monies. The market money of ticks is segregated from the dollars that can be used to buy food, entertainment, and durable objects. The Dow Jones Industrial Average (DJIA) consists in ticks measured in hundredth price increments. While the trader is in the pit, the trader does not refer to the dollar amount of the gain or loss. Only after leaving the space of the pit can this conversion be made legitimately: "Maintaining different names and accounting strategies for each currency divides the space of the market from the world outside the trading floor ... Accounting practices that separate market and social space allow traders to purify market calculations from outside considerations" (Zaloom 2006: 131). The purity of the market must be guarded through the mechanism of new market monies.

These cultural logics operate in the microinteractions of the trading floors. Notable characters make markets. In the local arena (or field) the traders await the maker whose arrival signals the start of the show. One bond trader used double entendre to inform Zaloom how a protagonist might arrive to warm and open up a frigid pit:

> When you're local, your job is to make a market. So make the damn market. What is [the bid/ask]? Give me a number. [Using the voice of a broker] "*I got a customer here who needs to be filled.*" When you get a cascading market or a rallying market, [the challenge is] who's going to be the first one to step in and say "*no more*"? Who's going to be the first one to say when the market is breaking?... OK, that's ... where the market is. Here is where it is going to stop. In the pit, you look to the guys that you know are going to be the ones to do it. You know when you are in the bond pit that everyone looks to Tom Baldwin ... There wouldn't have been a trade there without a local there to "*step up,*" that's what they call it on the floor. Who's going to step up and be the market? [emphasis added] (quoted in Zaloom 2006: 62)

Markets are made when real men "step up" and take charge. These gender codes and metaphorical understandings of what the bond pit is and how individuals can heat it up structure how individuals behave within it.

As traders enter the pits, they engage in a deeply personal, emotionally engrossing activity. Each understands first hand what loss feels like and each manages his perception of self by understanding how to take risks, how to suffer losses, and how to enjoy a winning trend. The trader engages bodily with the pen, the trading card, the screen, and other traders. The focus of attention and the emotional energy means that the actors engage in the game for the sake of profit, but they are also carried away by the game, whereby, one trader confessed, "You can experience the market and become a part of this living thing, intimately connected to it" (quoted in Zaloom 2006: 105).

The numbers (an exchange medium) on the computer screen become characters in their own right as traders watch them move in response to (and in the construction of) different narratives: "Numbers that halt a decline in the market are called 'support levels' and numbers that 'turn back a price advance' are attributed to powers of resistance. The numbers themselves in these statements are agents" (Zaloom 2006: 147). Certain round numbers (such as 10, 20, 25, 50, 75, 100, and multiples of 1,000) become symbolic markers, signaling to the traders the qualities of the trades and the direction of the performance. Traders look for signs before acting, and the shared expectations for what signs are appropriate before making a move create legitimacy for action and thereby reinforce each actor's judgment.

Household Monies

How households use money for a long time seemed mysterious. After all, if the head of household acted as if he had a single budget, he should have been able to allocate those monies efficiently to the household's needs. Instead, households operated as if they were little fiefdoms, each with their own, sometimes warring, priorities. People were making seemingly irrational decisions about how to spend money.

The Culture of Money and Prices

Viviana Zelizer has offered a way to piece together the puzzle of household budgeting. Instead of seeing money as fungible, usable for a variety of purposes, she sees money as marked for some purposes but not others. This is not merely an exercise of earmarking that is easily changed, given the household's needs. In the process of earmarking, the money itself is transformed into its own currency and restricted to a special purpose.

In her historical case study, Zelizer finds that a working-class woman had a completely different relationship with money and budgeting when compared with an upper-class woman. This difference was not due to how much money she had available but rather to the cultural codes about gender and social class that allowed the working-class woman to handle money, but not the upper-class woman. Even so, when a working-class woman brought her earnings into the household, they were used for different purposes compared with the earnings her husband collected. These monies constituted a new vocabulary of "allowance, pin money, 'egg money,' 'butter money,' spending money, pocket money, gift, or 'dole'" (Zelizer 1989: 344). Monies are identifiable by narrative and practice – by what they are called, where they are stored, how they are kept separate from the other (theoretically fungible) legal tender.

Moreover, in studies of immigrants, the money that women earned is spent differently than is the money earned by their husbands. Margarita Mooney (2003) and others have shown how some earnings are spent on school fees, school uniforms, groceries, and clothes, while other earnings (those of husbands) are spent on large appliances, trucks, and construction. It is not simply that women prioritize needs differently from men, but rather that money gets marked according to who earned it and how it was earned. The way money enters the household has much to do with how it will leave it.

Money is not merely a quantitative amount of legal tender deemed by the consumer as the equivalent (or less) of the good/ service being provided. Monies travel within a bundle of media, and it is the configuration of the bundle that makes the monies understandable to the grantor and the grantee. Some media bundles combine legal tender with tokens, points, or other credits. Other media bundles restrict an exchange to legal tender only, but this often happens as the legal tender itself has been transformed into an earmarked currency with restricted use. These restrictions are not imposed by the government but by the shared understanding that the user of the monies have for how the monies are supposed to be used in different situations. These media bundles become clear in the last section of this chapter where empirical examples highlight how media of exchange help to mark different definitions of market and non-market situations.

Money and Relational Work

Cultural understandings guide how people use money to bolster, challenge, or transform their interpersonal relationships. We will begin with money in intimate relationships because these examples help us think about business partnerships. When coupling and commerce mix, there are a variety of coupling types (categories of relationships) and many of the same "services" (acts) are exchanged across the coupling categories; however, the different categories of relationship are matched with different media of exchange. For instance, the traditional definition of dating consists in an event where the man spends money on the entertainment enjoyed by his companion and himself. He and his date may hold hands, hug, kiss, or provide one another with a variety of intimate services. For couples who are "going steady" there are a number of exchange media to mark their relationship type: "Going steady created its own characteristic matching of relations, transactions, and media. In general, the couple involved pooled resources far more than dating couples, typically planning their expenditures to assure their appearance at major social occasions ... [They] exchanged class rings, wore matching 'steady jackets,' or boys gave the girls a letter sweater" (Zelizer 2005: 115).

There are a number of relational categories in coupling such as "friends with benefits"; people who are "joined at the hip"; hanging out, dating, engagement, and more. There are also third parties who help to enforce the category of relationship. A ring that belonged to a man's mother will be blocked from exchange with someone he is merely dating and will be out of the question for a friend with benefits. Friends within one's social circle will ridicule or gossip about inappropriate gifts or unseemly exchanges, effectively sanctioning the transaction. The incessant negotiations about which media of exchange match what categories of relationship and the enforcement by third parties of the categorical boundaries constitute relational work.

It would be a mistake to assume that as intimacy increases so too does non-monetary exchange. This view is based on the notion that money corrupts intimacy, and it seems to make sense because one does not pay one's spouse cash for sex (dinner, a movie, and jewelry might be the preferred media of generalized exchange). Similarly, one does not write a check to one's husband or wife for house cleaning or yard work, although money might exchange hands for a non-family member performing the same tasks. By contrast, Zelizer writes, couples intending to marry may begin to give one another large amounts of cash and may also begin to share expenses along with a bank account. This increase in monetary exchanges does not mean that market media (money) have corrupted the relationship or that the couple has become less intimate. Instead, the increased monetary exchanges signal an increasing trust between the individuals, marking them as a bounded unit.

Even among various forms of commercial sex work do we find a number of distinctions being made about the type of commercial sex that is being purchased. Zelizer describes the taxi-dance halls of the 1920s and 1930s as a "complex economy of favors, gifts, tips, and obligation" (Zelizer 2005: 120). This was not simply the commodification of intimacy and a straightforward story of exploitation. There were standard transactions in which the man paid for his dance by purchasing drinks and cash payments for dance-hall tickets. A good customer would sometimes be granted a free dance. If the dancer became his mistress, cash became less important as he spent money on rent, groceries, and clothes to mark the changed nature of their relationship, and this change in the media exchange bundles also happened with women who would stay overnight with their men. Even the timing between when a woman might ask for money and when she had engaged in sex with the man mattered so that the sexual acts could be decoupled from the gifts of cash and the category of the relationship could remain unchallenged as being about more than just money. This required a finely executed dance not easily choreographed.

Likewise, business partnership takes on the character of a choreographed dance, with some dancers commandingly taking the lead, others stepping on their partner's toes. In *The New Old Economy* (2005), Josh Whitford examines manufacturing companies in the Midwest and uses the language of the waltz to describe what the various parties to a negotiation or to a business partnership are trying to do. Whitford begins with the Original Equipment Manufacturer (OEM), those companies that can produce the final product at their facility by relying on other companies to source parts, materials, and as-needed expertise. This means that the OEM is the lead firm and that it calls in other players to very specific inputs in some cases, but in other cases there are brainstorming sessions or ambiguity over what the needed inputs will be. Many of the contractors are not intimate friends with the chief operating officer or the key negotiators for the lead firm, but they nonetheless engage in collaborative relationships. This at first seemed to be contradictory collaboration, but Whitford (2012) has since come to define it as contested collaboration, and in its status as contested, the exchange of money and other media as well as constant negotiations about what those exchanges mean (relational work) enable these OEMs to operate well.

Money and Boundary Work

Consider some widespread narratives about people's character based on how they use money and what they do with prices. According to Frederick Wherry (2008), prices are not culturally neutral but are used to compare the qualities of differently situated people, those near to versus those far from the mainstream. He argues that consumers become characterized as foolish, faithful, frivolous, or frugal by virtue of how they seem to be evaluating the prices of goods and services, but that these valuations differ not only by the types of goods and services being purchased but also by the identity (and social location) of the purchaser. These characterizations are consequential for societal assessments about what differently characterized consumers deserve.

One could imagine extending these insights into the current housing crisis in the United States. The epidemic of mortgage defaults resulted from a complex financial set of instruments that allowed banks to take unjustified risks; however, the popular understanding of what happened is that foolish people made bad decisions, while frugal people are left to suffer the long-term consequences (loss of wealth). If an individual happens to go into default on her loan, how will she be regarded by the societal mainstream? Wherry would argue that this will depend on how near-to or far-from the mainstream she is. If she is a member of a marginalized minority group, her defaulting on a loan is more likely to be judged as foolishness rather than bad luck, whatever the circumstances of the case. People make snap judgments about how others ended up in their current situations, and these judgments color their understandings of what should be done about another's misfortune.

David Harvey (2010) noticed that when the sub-prime crisis only seemed to affect working-class people of color (far from the mainstream), it was not a crisis, but when foreclosures reached white, middle-class households, it became a moral matter of good people being duped by complicated instruments rather than another instance in which a fool and her money were soon parted. These boundaries between the deservingly and the undeservingly duped could be extended to the deserving and undeserving bailouts. There were public expressions of disgust toward unionized industries that found themselves bankrupt and in need of assistance from the public's purse, and the emphasis lay in greedy, undeserving workers who had tried to transform otherwise profitable industries into welfare hotels. These symbolic boundaries help predict durable inequalities and are not merely the consequences of unequal material conditions.

What is important to keep in mind is that what economic actors do is not evaluated in a vacuum, nor is it understandable outside of the relative identity of the actor. A person is understood to have qualities that are similar-to or different-from other people. People sort themselves and become sorted into groups according to their similarities to or differences from other "stock characters" (in the dramaturgical sense) in the marketplace. The horizon of possibilities differs by character type, and these characters enact their social personalities by taking on, talking about, and demonstrating their relationship with culturally significant prices. In their play with prices, people erect symbolic boundaries between themselves and others.

Conclusion

Among economic sociologists, Viviana Zelizer (2010) has led the charge in rejecting theories of money that do not attend to the diversity of monetary practices that people have used over time and the diversity of outcomes money has had on personal relationships and on the power dynamics of people within households. She calls for an interpretive social science that attends to what people actually do and what they feel about what they are doing. She shows how variable-oriented theories of what money is and how it works do not reflect existing historical records and ethnographic accounts of money and other exchange media. Behavioral psychologists (concerned with what people actually do and why) agree that the meanings of money have consequences for how it is used. It would be a mistake, however, to assume that meanings matter only in the emotionally drenched realm of households. Even the legal tender of nation-states and world regions communicate symbols, stories, and meanings that people are willing to fight for. In money and prices we find abundant empirical materials for the study of culture and economic life.

4

How to Conduct Cultural Analyses
of Markets

The previous chapters have sketched how culture affects the
organization of markets and how consumers come to understand how they should act in an economic transaction as well
as what they should want. This chapter will demonstrate how
one engages in cultural analyses of markets and of economic
processes using historical methods, the analysis of images and
narratives, and direct observation (ethnography). Common
sense understandings about the laws of the market discourage
empirical investigations into them; after all, if the tendency of
individuals is to optimize benefits while minimizing costs, studying whether and how groups of people participate in markets
seems futile. Following this line of thinking, one can only learn
what one already knows; mathematical models tell all. This
book has offered a number of propositions about where our
economic categories of thought come from and how those categories of thought vary from one group to another. The studies
summarized here have also demonstrated that the way people
think about markets affect what they do in them. How do we
know that these alternative explanations are right? How much
confidence should we have in cultural analyses of markets (reliability)? And how can one ensure that one's interpretation of
why groups of people behave as they do corresponds with what
those people think they are doing (validity)?

To engage in cultural analysis is to focus on meanings. In some cases, the analyst concerns herself with what causes a particular set of meanings to emerge. In other cases, the analyst concentrates on how meanings affect specific outcomes. For example, one might ask what causes an idea to seem innovative or what causes a group to participate in savings more than consumption or to prefer investing in the stock market to depositing money into a savings account? These ideas about what is innovative or what preferred may have less to do with the amounts and types of information available to groups of individuals than it has to do with what innovation means and what the stock market means for individuals who are members of an identifiable social group (neighborhood community, ethnic group, type of migrant, or the type of family the individual heads). One might also ask how ways of thinking tend to be similar within groups and how these ways of thinking account for how people within those groups behave. Analysts studying entire societies, countries, or industries ask similar questions, such as why the same industry is organized differently in several different countries with the same access to information, technology, and financial resources.

In this chapter we start with historical methods because they help us see in hindsight how economic arrangements did not have to be as they are. Historical methods open up the range of possibilities in market logics and in market configurations that most people take for granted. Then we move to image and narrative analysis before turning to ethnography. These methods help us see what types of behaviors and taken-for-granted rules lead to specific market outcomes as well as the multiple purposes that marketplaces serve.

Historical Methods

Historians ramble through stacks of memoranda, letters, pamphlets, policy papers, and texts in order to establish what happened, where, when, and among whom; what did the event mean for differently situated persons (for insiders versus outsiders; buyers versus sellers); and what were the overarching understandings about how the event should have unfolded versus how it was actually played out. Social historians tell us how entire industries change and what the collective narratives were facilitating particular types of change. There are material and ideational trends to be established; from the former, one determines the number of companies that existed over a period of time and how the reported profits rose sharply at a specific time or declined precipitously; then one asks whether the public discourse (an indicator of cultural understandings) changed prior to, during, or after the industry's founding or its change in fortune.

A well-known example of this approach can be found in Viviana Zelizer's examination of life insurance companies. They began to grow after the 1840s and became well established by the 1870s. Dissatisfied with conventional economic and demographic explanations for the growth and establishment of the life insurance market, Zelizer offered a cultural history of the market to establish what the cultural conditions were before, during, and after the market's rise. She identified publications published by insurance companies that offer justifications for life insurance and that respond to objections from customers and from civic organizations concerned with the effects of putting a monetary price on life (generating "dirty money" or "profane money"); insurance companies also had to respond to superstitious beliefs about how preparing for death might hasten it. The publications include *The United States Insurance Gazette, Insurance Journal*, and *Life Insurance* (controlled by the Manhattan Life Insurance Company), among others. In these publications the insurance companies have identified and attempted to contend with the prevailing cultural understandings that impede the take-off of the insurance market, while highlighting those cultural beliefs that foster it.

Because these documents are published periodically, Zelizer can identify changes in discourse *over time*. And she can also consider the economic and demographic conditions that sometimes shape (but at other times are shaped by) these dominant cultural discourses. As she pays close attention to *when* cultural explanations are given, extolled, or confronted, she marks the temporal order in which changes in cultural understandings *precede* changes in the insurance market. Her findings are unexpected: when insurance companies tried to reject cultural understandings and rituals believed to be impediments to it, the market did not thrive; however, when insurance companies began to embrace the rituals associated with death and the cultural understandings of the "good death" (along with the distinctions between sacred and profane money), the insurance market flourished.

Social scientists concerned with reliability want to know whether another scientist studying the same phenomenon would more-or-less come up with the same conclusions. A variety of details may slightly contradict or overly enforce the main story-line told by the historian. The question becomes whether the main story-line holds; whether the historian exhaustively examined the available documents from the time-period and how she handled evidence that contradicts her thesis. What is the universe of available texts; why do some texts survive but others not?

These questions cannot always be satisfactorily answered nor must they. Cultural histories rely on what Robert K. Merton calls "strategic research materials" – situations where otherwise hard to pinpoint social forces manifest themselves with remarkable clarity. For example, an industry dealing with life and death issues more obviously brings questions of the sacred to the fore, even in a capitalist market. And cultural histories – strategically selected – need not depend on a representative sample of life insurance companies. A deeply investigated set of focal actors and organizations in the insurance market will allay fears that a follow-up investigation of what happened by whom (along with when and where) would reliability yield similar results.

The question of validity is more bedeviling: Are we measuring what we think we are measuring? In *The Interpretation of Cultures* Clifford Geertz uses the example of a wink versus a twitch to illustrate how "thin" observations may seem at first to be objective and therefore best capable of examining the social world, but reliability observed actions may falsely render what is actually going on.

> Consider... two boys rapidly contracting the eyelids of their right eyes. In one, this is an involuntary twitch; in the other, a conspiratorial signal to a friend. The two movements are, as movements, identical; from an I-am-a-camera, ... Yet the difference ... between a twitch and a wink is vast ... Contracting your eyelids on purpose when there exists a public code in which so doing counts as a conspiratorial signal *is* winking. That's all there is to it: a speck of behavior, a fleck of culture, and – *voilá* – a gesture. (Geertz [1973] 2000: 6)

The analysts must establish what the existing public codes are, what the context of the action is, and how the type of situation the individual is in determine the meaning of the gesture. To the extent that the analyst establishes what the existing public codes and collective narratives are using existing findings and her own understanding of the materials at hand, she has offered a conceptually valid rendering of meaningful behaviors. Because a community of scientists can interrogate the existing research that has helped the historian make her interpretations and because this same community of scholars can judge the historical materials to be reasonable, relative to the types and the volume of materials gathered for other historical studies of the same type, we can have confidence that the historian's interpretations of what happened and why are conceptually valid.

Our sense of validity increases as the number of cases grows. Sociologists Margaret Somers and Fred Block examine "welfare revolutions" across space and time, using the method of agreement to establish the causal importance of ideas for shaping economic policies. Because the two cases differ in every way except for the outcome of interest and for the independent variable predicting it, the comparative study is especially amenable to the method of agreement. Rather than two countries (similar in size, political structure, and economic conditions) experiencing these revolutions in roughly the same time-period, these authors compare a revolution in England in 1834 where the New Poor Law represented the triumph of market fundamentalism and a publicly hailed revolution in the United States where the Personal Responsibility and Work Opportunities Reconciliation Act had largely the same functional effect in the public's understanding about what causes poverty and what responsibilities tax payers and their governments have in addressing it.

The materials they use (establishing from where the warring sets of ideas come) include the memoranda, white papers (policy position papers), and proclamations published by the Royal Commission in 1834 in England and the Domestic Policy Council's Low Income Opportunity Working Group in the United States, labor statutes and discussions of labor and poverty by public intellectuals and well known philosophers. They also include writings by prominent public policy analysts. This variation in where the materials come from challenges the analyst to justify why the ideas expressed in these data sources reflect the dominant ideas of the time-period. The effectiveness of cultural history does not depend on whether a data source is complete (e.g. does not have years in which a periodical or memorandum is missing) or representative (e.g. whether a majority of the public or a majority of the politicians or business owners concerned with a particular problem would agree that the materials analyzed are the most frequently read by policymakers, voters, or by a large segment of relevant consumers). It is not the frequency with which an object or word is used but its meaningful significance that the analyst must interpret. In this way, cultural history, like psychiatry, is a tinkering trade.

As historians, sociologists, and anthropologists tinker with the facts of a case, they develop biographies of people, places, and things. It is the biography of things, whether they be monies or goods, follow a developmental arc. Things are born; they mature; they sometimes have stunted growth; they may die and be re-born. According to Igor Kopytoff (1986), one finds such biographies in the histories of commercial goods. If one follows when an object was not circulating in the commercial marketplace and at what moment it became possible to think about an object as suitable for purchase (exchange value) or suitable as a medium of exchange (money), one is capturing the object's commodity biography. In each stage of life (commodity phase), the commodity undergoes what Arjun Appadurai (1986: 13–15) calls its commodity candidacy within its commodity context. Its candidacy refers to whether the object can be bought or sold, in the first place. Its context refers to the meaningful social arena in which the exchanges occur. In its commodity candidacy, an object may undergo rites of passage from the sacred to the profane or may linger in a tainted middle stage. Some sacred objects defy pricing logics altogether and remain priceless, though priced (e.g. the insurance value of a child's life [Zelizer 1989] or the well-known painting hanging in the Louvre [Appadurai 1986]). Other objects are infused with meaning, keeping their scarcity high along with their prices. These histories of goods necessarily involve an understanding of how the culture of the markets in which these goods circulate changes along with how understandings of what these goods are and how they should be used are transformed.

Image and Narrative Analysis

Markets are full of images: company logos and emblems, the covers of travel books, tourism maps, advertisements, company websites, and the covers of quarterly reports. Markets are also replete with narratives explaining the logos, the cultural and historical significance of places, persons, and things to international tourists, the worth of a brand, or the reverence held for the founding fathers or mothers of a firm. Some cultural analysts dig into a single set of images and texts from a single time-period; from this cross-section of materials the analyst interprets meaning and thinks through what the images and texts do not say but that could be said, given the other things we know about a company, a place, a person, or a product. Other cultural analysts choose instead to follow images, emblems, logos, brands, and founding stories *over time*. Similar to the historical sociologists discussed in this chapter, these cultural analysts ask how meanings have changed and why; they also enquire into the consequences (economic and otherwise) of those changes.

Cultural geographers and marketers studying the Thai tourism industry, for example, have looked at the maps of places like Bangkok and noted the extent to which bars, red-light districts, brothels, and nightlife are emphasized on the map relative to the cultural heritage of the country (its temples, monuments, and museums) (see ch. 1 in Bandelj and Wherry 2011; Casino and Hanna 2000; Nuttavuthisit 2007). These same analysts have looked at attempts by the Thai Tourism Authority to manage impressions that outsiders have of the country and how these attempts are reflected on the covers of the tourism guidebooks. Where exotic women holding a cocktail while lounging on the beach dominated earlier covers, more recent covers show monks in saffron robes, gold leafed temples, classical Thai dancers engaged in court dances. The shift in images has come with a shift in the type of tourism and the types of market offerings local Thai businesses now promote. As the analyst moves through the images over time, she can comment on what gets erased, what gets highlighted, and what political struggles behind the scenes led to particular images being portrayed with less emphasis, less frequency.

Within an industry or a country, there is a remarkable convergence of images and of story themes. When image types and story themes begin to change, they often start changing at the same time, in response to similar social or cultural crises in society. It is the job of the analyst to figure out what the critical discourse moment is, when a new set of themes emerged as salient for promoting the same place, product, or service (or when an existing set of themes precipitously declined in importance). These moments become the triggers of change in the meaning systems that give these symbols and stories their power; and these moments are not merely shifts in material reality, because sometimes the material reality changes little but the meaningful narratives begin to change and lead to changes in the deeply held cultural understandings groups of people have about a place, a thing, a person, or a set of action strategies.

Most scholars can agree that the analysis of images or texts can be done in a replicable way; for example, one can count how many times a specific set of images appear in one time-period versus another or how often a phrase shows up to describe an industry or a destination site. In this way, there are findings from image and narrative analysis that can be reliably obtained from other researchers who do not have the same interpretive inclinations, but the question becomes whether it is a worthy exercise to conduct counts without an assessment of what a word or an image mean. Clifford Geertz said it best when he quipped, "It is not worth it, as Thoreau said, to go round the world to count the cats of Zanzibar" (Geertz [1973] 2001: 16). The power of these analyses lies in what these images or narratives mean and how they reflect established, contestable, or contested notions about what roles people ought to play, what attributes people, places, and things surely have, or how things ought to be done.

For an example of how images and narratives can be fruitfully analyzed, let's turn to Douglas Holt, a sociologist who teaches in a marketing department. He argues that cultural disruptions in society enable a brand to resonate with consumers. If cultural codes about what it means to be a man are in flux, there will be a turning point in how men psychologically connect with products like the Harley Davidson motorcycle. It is not the product that is changing or the material conditions of society that are rendering the Harley more or less desirable for the target audience; instead, it is the sense that a set of cultural codes have been ruptured and need to be re-established and/ or reconstructed that leads to the discursive turning point. Savvy marketers try to stay attuned to these cultural ruptures so that they know when and how to change their marketing messages.

Likewise, Lauren Rivera, another sociologist teaching at a business school, has studied how presentation teams in a governmental tourism promotion office engage in what Erving Goffman calls impression management, as the team concerns itself with what aspects of its identity might be stigmatizing and how best to deal with those attributes. Because the tourism office produces a yearly tourism brochure, Rivera could look at how the image of the country has changed over time, and she chose to do this with the case of Croatia. She could ask of the text: what are the relevant comparison groups for the country's cultural heritage, its architecture, and its geography? How do these descriptions render the same architecture as being near-to the Europeans in one time-period but far-from the Europeans in another? Lauren Rivera's coding strategy indicates where the descriptions of Croatia's cultural heritage reference European, local, Turkish/Ottoman, or a mix of origins:

Culture: European ... EXAMPLE: "Croatian culture forms an integral part of West European culture."

Culture: Local ... EXAMPLE: "Istria is noted for its own unique culture, music and quite specific cuisine, all of which made it widely known for being a wondrous and magical land."

Culture: Turkish/Ottoman ... EXAMPLE: "Oriental influenced exoticism of cultural life."

Culture: Mixed ... EXAMPLE: "Croatia has stood for centuries on the very border of Western and Eastern cultural influences." (Rivera 2008: A6)

Although the geography of the country has not physically changed, its symbolic geography has. Sometimes Croatia is situated in the Balkans; at other times, more generally in Eastern Europe; then Western Europe; then the Mediterranean.

These changes in the depiction of a single place are intentional acts, meant to make a place more attractive for the tourism and the foreign direct investment markets, yet the marketers and the impression management teams are aware that they cannot depict a place in any way that they wish. There are prior understandings, collective stories, and comparison places that most outsiders already associate as being similar to or different from the country in question. Rivera shows that the comparison countries and traditions do change over time; therefore, the reputational work of marketers is not bound in land, asphalt, or architecture for all time. How some of this reputational work gets carried out, however, cannot be understood while looking at images and narratives alone. This requires the observation of people engaged in reputational acts at close range.

Ethnographic Methods

Ethnography refers to the science of observation. In direct observation, the observer is detached from the action at hand;

113

for example, she may act as a spectator watching people interact and talk about prices in different buying situations, but he may not participate in the action as a buyer, a seller, or a consultant who potentially sways the outcomes of the transaction, or she may visit a variety of auctions in order to understand what the rules seem to be that govern how prices are set for different goods, or why the price of the same good varies in different selling situations. By contrast, as a participant observer, the observer also engages in the activities he observers: she may work as a trader on the floor of the stock exchange in order to understand what rules people follow that are not clearly indicated in their work contracts but that are collectively understood as the way business ought to be done. She may work as a sales clerk in a fair trade shop interacting with customers and getting to know franchise owners in order to understand how sellers and buyers justify the higher prices they pay for fair trade products.

Ethnographers write field notes, descriptions of what happened, where, when, by whom, and for what reasons. Over time, the ethnographer has a written record that shows how a person, a group, place, or phenomenon has changed over time. Like a psychiatrist, the ethnographer tries to identify the patterns of behavior exhibited by the person or the group. With whom are they friendly and with whom hostile? When talking about specific subjects, what issues are usually raised and which ones are taken-for-granted (ignored) versus placed off limits (prohibited, due to taboo)? With each encounter the ethnographer gets a thicker description of the person, group, or phenomenon she is studying.

The ethnographic analysis of markets proceeds in three steps: (1) the ethnographer determines what will be observed and to what it will be compared; (2) the ethnographer sketches the scene, noting the usual locations of people and things in the scene; (3) the ethnographer listens to the conversations that people have in the scene, the nicknames they give each other and the special names they give to behaviors and to objects; and (4) the ethnographer repeats these steps in order to understand how behaviors change (or remain the same) in a single scene or how behaviors differ between scenes. At each step of the way, the ethnographer must ask what the setting means for the people in it, what the special names and specialized language means, and what seems to be the intent of peoples' actions.

When Charles Smith wrote *Auctions*, he wrote that the marketplace is a stage and that the buyers and sellers are merely players. Smith visited a variety of auctions and began by simply describing the scenes and what people wore to the auctions. Although Smith does not observe a representative sample of auctions, his findings are nonetheless valid. Smith does not claim that these meaningful dynamics are unfolding in the exact same way across all auctions of a particular type, but he is offering us some heuristic tools for looking at the meaningful dimensions of market exchange and how these collective norms and stories constrain market action.

Even if Smith had followed only a few individuals as they engaged in routine shopping, he would have uncovered some insights into the culture of shopping. Analogously, when Sigmund Freud engaged in his interpretive analyses of single individuals and their meaningful life stories, he developed insights about the role of taboo in social life. Sociologist George Steinmetz defends the close examination of a single ethnographic or historical case by noting the advances in psychoanalysis and literary criticism:

> In a field like psychoanalysis, for instance, the case study is just as important as more abstract theoretical interventions in driving theoretical development forward. Within literary criticism, the interpretation of particular texts is as central to theoretical development as comparative studies (or abstract theoretical interventions). By the same token, the case study of a specific social event, process, or community is as important a part of the overall sociological enterprise as comparison or sustained theoretical

reflection. *The plausibility of a given theoretical argument can be assessed only by studying complex, overdetermined, empirical objects (particular individual psychobiographies, specific practices and so on).* [emphasis added] (Steinmetz 2004: 383)

Narratives do not need to be reduced to variables or to a few parsimonious factors to make them scientifically useful. Thick description enables the radical uprooting of phenomena from familiar terrain so that these phenomena may be interrogated for the structures (cultural and material) that shape and invigorate the phenomena under investigation.

Consider how cultural discourses and power dynamics impinge on the consumption lives of racial minorities who are economically disadvantaged. Anthropologist Elizabeth Chin observes ten-year-old, black kids over a two-year period and collects consumption journals that these kids kept. Chin explains how they make decisions about purchases and how they put these purchases to use in maintaining and contesting the types of relationships they are in, the decisions that the young people make *in the moment* as well as her observations about how they make purchases, with whom, with what type of gait, demeanor, gesture, and cadence. When a young boy agonizes over a toy that can be easily shared and one that would be for his singular use, he is orienting his purchase decision to a web of social relationships where his purchase will be assessed. And as these young people enter shopping spaces, they identify and respond to the discursive binary of white/black, freedom/slavery, buyer/borrower, and creative/destructive. From her thick description of what the kids do, Chin captures the "codes, narratives, and symbols that create the textured webs of social meaning" (Alexander and Smith 2003: 13).

It is instructive to see how Chin uses objects to elicit the meanings that purchases have for her research subjects. These are not experiments carefully designed but moments of opportunity wisely seized.

I spied a frazzle-haired Barbie doll beneath Natalia's seat and, holding my tape recorder, asked the girls to tell me about Barbie ... Natalia and Asia delivered a dialogue keenly expressing their sense of cultural and social location:

ASIA You never see a fat Barbie. You never see a pregnant Barbie. What about those things? They should make a Barbie that can have a baby.

NATALIA Yeah...and make a fat Barbie. So when we play Barbie... you could be a fat Barbie.

ASIA Okay. What I was saying that Barbie... how can I say this? They make her like a stereotype ... You never, ever... think of an abused Barbie. (Chin 2001: 1–2)

Many middle-class children cannot imagine pregnancy being germane to a Barbie doll, given her age, her status as unmarried, and her future ambitions. The range of possibilities for Barbie differs by the cultural and material worlds these children inhabit. The object (a doll) is the same for middle-class as for poor, and working-class kids, but the lens through which the kids understand what happens to a pretty girl differ dramatically.

Because Chin has followed and established rapport with these young girls, she is able to ask them questions and to capture their responses on her tape recorder. She is also able to observe how they perform their responses for the tape, assuming an Oprah-like persona and dramatically pausing to convey affect. It is this horizon of meaning that illuminates how cultural codes about class, race, and gender work through consumption.

Christine Williams shows how studying shopping spaces can shed light on how race, class, and gender work. Williams engages in participant observation of two toy stores, selected not because they "represent" typical stores but because they enable her to see these dynamics in a upper-income versus a working-class context. She begins by observing how the stores are laid out and who works where on the shopping floor. The spatial layout resembles Cook's historical analysis of shopping where he judiciously uses floor maps, but she supplements the spatial organization of the shopping floor with the social organization of its workers on it. The Asian men work in electronics, the men work in the back stocking (with the exception of one woman who is considered to be a butch lesbian), the lighter complexioned and younger African-American women work the cash register. How customers interact with these different characters on the floor illuminates racial and class dynamics and helps Williams to examine how racial and gender inequalities are reproduced in the course of routine shopping excursions.

Keeping Cultural Analyses Cultural

Mario Small argues that trying to make qualitative research "fit" the approach and standards of quantitative research will lessen the scientific value of qualitative research. Like a language poorly translated, the meanings, pitch, and cadence can be lost. Researchers who want to make cultural analyses "more scientific" might make the mistake of ignoring ethnographic observation and the testimonials of a few key informants in favor of data obtained from a random representative sample of respondents.

Following the advice of King, Keohane, and Verba (1994), some cultural analyses of markets attempt to find a "representative" firm or a "typical" market setting so that the findings can inform work in similar settings. Is the firm the average or median size in terms of profits or staff? Is the market setting one with consumers who are not at the very high or the very low end of the income distribution? And if these consumers are extremely rich or extremely poor, do they "represent" their respective socio-economic class? Asking these questions can be helpful for managing a research study and for making decisions that quantitatively oriented analysts understand, but these approaches do not enable the researcher to generate conclusions that can be generalized to a population of firms or of market settings, if we take Frankfort-Nachmias and Nachmias's (2000: 167 cited in Small 2009: 16) definition of representativeness: "[A] sample is considered representative if the analyses made using the sampling units produce results similar to those that would be obtained had the entire population been analyzed." A single firm does not constitute such a sample, nor does a single market setting.

King, Keohane, and Verba (1994) have suggested that small "samples" compensate for their size by going deep, with in-depth interviews and extended periods of observation. Suppose we chose one firm with standard characteristics for its industry-size: a large toy manufacturer with 43 executives and 3,000 employees (Morrill 1995). Suppose we interviewed the head of the firm for a total of twenty hours over the course of two years. And we interviewed the staff and observed them interact with one another over the course of a year. No matter how copious our notes might be, we could have little confidence that what we saw happening in this one firm was being loosely replicated in any of the two hundred or two thousand firms it is said to "represent."

Now, let's suppose that the researcher took a case- (rather than a variable-) oriented approach and chose a firm that has adopted a new matrix system of management. How does the firm's inhabitants deal with conflict in this new system? As we thickly described the imagery being used in the firm, the character distinctions made between different executives as honorable or not, and the rituals performed before, during, and after specific types of conflict, we overturn erroneous understandings of individuals as robots who focus their attentions on making more money and for whom rituals and symbols matter little. Only by uncovering the life world of the firm can we begin to understand what motivates action and why the firm's agents may appear to be mixed up about why they have come to work, engaging in inefficient, non-productive behaviors.

Small reminds us of the value of case studies that examine the exceptional or the extraordinary. While these cases do not result from a random sample or from a place with similar characteristics to other places, they nonetheless provide researchers with strategic research materials. Such materials, Robert Merton (1957) notes, enable the researcher to see sociological processes with remarkable clarity – a vision denied under the usual conditions. If a community organization decided to use the neighborhood's ethnic identity and cultural heritage in the service of economic development, that organization's leadership might be said to be exceptional, charismatic, and perhaps even lucky. The varied responses to these efforts by people within and outside of the community depend on a number of factors, making the success or failure of the case difficult to explain parsimoniously. The case is "over-determined" because it is real.

Downplaying the value of parsimony, Michael Burawoy proposes a reflexive model of science that recognizes the value of capturing how people experience the world. He argues that the structures underlying daily life do not reside in the imagination of the researcher but somewhere between the analyst's thoughtful engagement with theory and her observations of and participation in that life. And finding the balance between the two has important pay-offs in studying how and why people follow somewhat predictable patterns of behavior.

> I hope to demonstrate that reflexive science has its pay-off, enabling the exploration of broad historical patterns and macrostructures *without* relinquishing either ethnography or science. By ethnography I mean writing about the world from the standpoint of participant observation. In developing my argument it will be necessary to distinguish (a) research *method* (here survey research and the extended case method), which is the deployment of (b) *techniques* of empirical investigation (here interviewing and participant

observation) to best approximate (c) a scientific *model* (positive or reflexive) that lays out the presuppositions and principles for producing science. (Burawoy 1998: 6)

Both Burawoy and George Steinmetz argue for a different model of science that focuses less on large data-sets and more on meaningful experiences and step-by-step processes.

Through participant observation the analyst imperfectly excavates the social structures impinging on social and cultural life. By honing in on the unique, the analyst can glimpse the general, and theory makes it possible. The researcher builds on theory by zigzagging between it and the empirical case observed at close range. Burawoy "extends out" from specific case studies to make claims about broad sociological processes and recognizes that these extensions lack statistical significance. To understand how capitalism works in postcolonial Africa, for example, the Manchester School of social anthropologists developed theoretically informed case studies of what native people were actually doing, what meanings they imbued in their actions and in their relationships, and how they negotiated and struggled over principles and over outcomes. These studies linked what was happening in a single factory, for example to the broader historical contexts, illuminating how colonial political structures and economic systems affect the possibilities for resistance on the factory floor. Following this line of thinking, C. K. Lee (1998) examines cultural codes and gendered practices in China to illustrate how labor markets too have collective understandings that hinder (or facilitate) political mobilizations for better pay and better working conditions.

Markets work well because cultural discourse and power dynamics make them seem as if they are naturally occurring and as if their normal participants share a similar instrumentally rational propensity to truck, barter, and trade. Cultural discourse does not emanate solely from the interests of capital, the manipulation of cultural dupes, or the material necessities for survival. Cultural effects work well because they often fail to provide obvious manifestations of themselves. Like power effects, cultural effects attend to the negations, disavowals, and foreclosures leading economic actors to enact scripts and to move as if by instinct – referencing core beliefs while acting upon them.

To identify cultural effects, strategies of action that are effective versus those that fall flat, the vocabularies of power, and the micropolitics of power that depend upon cultural discursive structures, one would need to be able to enter into a firm, for example, and be exempted from the conditions of confidentiality and from the concerns that proprietary information might be divulged in a full excavation of the dynamics within the firm.

Pierre Bourdieu (2005: 218) recognizes how hard it is to study firms and other private sector actors. He himself did this in a case study of a cement firm located in Paris in 1986. He wanted to show how people within the cement firm battled over defining what the official functions were of the different parts of the firm and how decisionmaking power should change among the firm's departments and its leaders. By virtue of what was done in the previous time-period, actions in the current or the future time-period would be made to seem "obvious" – a natural response to changing market conditions. What Bourdieu wants to demonstrate is that if one follows the definitional battles within the firm, it becomes clear that the obvious, natural response to the market depends heavily on these definitional battles. The difficulty comes in showing hard evidence that some actors purposefully worked to change the rules of the game so that their own power would increase (and that there were colorful rituals that facilitated decisionmaking). How can such hard evidence be presented without violating confidentiality vows?

> Although the conditions of confidentiality in which the research was carried out prevent us from chronicling in detail the countless

interventions (including, in particular, what one informant called the "billiard games," in which one person was played off against another) and the negotiations, or even from listing the strategies deployed – particularly to impose a policy or win acceptance for acceptance of it by inducing the chief executive to decide in its favor – we can at least speak of the logic of the struggle within the field of power in the firm... (Bourdieu 2005: 218)

In quantitative data analysis, some questions cannot be asked because data cannot be verified or its confidentiality cannot be insured. Bourdieu insists on breaking out of the straightjacket of quantitative methodology by noting that there are some things that can be discovered through unorthodox research strategies (being on site and sometimes undercover). The fact that the rules of confidentiality prevent the presentation of evidence in an orthodox way should not prevent the analysts from explaining their findings, especially when it enables our understanding of how firms work and why markets have the outcomes that are so consequential.

Conclusion

This chapter has tried to demystify what is meant by cultural analysis so that students of culture and markets can launch new studies, building on the insights of others. It might seem difficult to analyze the culture of markets given that collective narratives can be so powerful as to convince individuals that they behave in ways (and for reasons) that direct observation contradicts; moreover, the power of collective narratives and shared understandings remain hidden from individuals who do not see how their private lives are shaped by public issues. As far as they are concerned, they have made individual choices based on the information they had at hand and on their interests at maximizing the benefits of their action. They do not see how their social ties to other people, the beliefs that people have about what should have happened in the transaction, or their own beliefs about the value of persons and things (independent of the use and the exchange value of those persons and things) shape market outcomes. As cultural analysts, it is our task to analyze the haze of meanings that enable people to justify why they do what they do, and it is also our duty to engage respectfully with these meanings.

In contrast to the previous chapters that have explained how cultural sociologists understand demand, supply, and transactions, this chapter has focused on the mechanics and the logics of analysis. What are the steps that historical sociologists take to understand the meanings of markets? What are the steps that other qualitative researchers take, and what are the strengths and weaknesses of these approaches? If *The Culture of Markets* succeeds, it is because it explains not only why culture matters but also how to investigate culture at work. The future investigations are left to you.

Conclusion: Toward a Cultural Sociology of Markets

After being belittled as an epiphenomenon of markets, culture has emerged as one of its critical predictors. Sociologists, anthropologists, and behavioral psychologists have turned to the culture of markets to explain what information access, network ties, years of education, prior work experience, and existing endowments of material resources won't; namely why there is so much variation in how people change within, act upon, and evaluate markets. Nina Bandelj (2008), for example, combines interviews with investors and quantitative data on economic and human capital conditions, to explain that some countries in Central Eastern Europe attracted significantly more foreign direct investment than comparable neighbors by virtue of the cultural affinities the investors had. Joel Podolny (2005) predicts which firms will partner with one another, based on their status within a community of firms. Frederick Wherry (2007) looks at the cultural politics of nation-states to understand the differential supports that their cultural industries receive and the reputations that their producers have in the global marketplace. And behavioral psychologists Amos Tversky and Daniel Kahneman (1981) emphasize how meaning differs from math as individuals evaluate the gains and losses resulting from their financial decisions; meanwhile, in *Identity Economics* (2010), George

Akerlof and Rachel Kranton have brought key insights from sociology about the role of identity and norms in shaping how people behave in markets. Many of these wide-ranging insights are inspired by and captured in a recent collection by one of economic sociology's founders, Viviana Zelizer (2010), who explains how culture shapes household, local, and larger economies.

As cultural approaches to the economy have intensified, so too have concerns with linking the theoretical developments in cultural sociology with those in economic sociology and related fields. Unlike economic sociology, cultural sociology has not traditionally focused on "economic" topics but rather on meaning making, dramaturgical performances in interpersonal encounters, and the categories that order social life. By contrast, culturally inflected studies within economic sociology have increasingly taken these theoretical tools from cultural sociology (and sociology more generally) to explain the meanings of economic action, the meanings of money, dramaturgical performances within market encounters, and the categories that order economic behavior.

The *spirit of calculation* (Bourdieu 2000: 25) is not universal but a historically contingent understanding collectively shared in a society. Economic ideas that most people take for granted (money, credit, saving, spending, wage work, etc.) are embodied beliefs and economic dispositions that influence what and how people understand goods to be goods and what people do with their money and their goods. In Pierre Bourdieu's investigation of Algerian workers after their country was liberated from French colonization, he excavated the "folk economics" of a cook to demonstrate that the economic ethos of modern capitalism differs from the ethos of the earlier period and that such dispositions as economic rationality and allocation efficiency (that minimizes costs and maximizes profits) were historically constituted.

To work for a wage, to obtain goods on credit, to have

confidence in credit cards, and to feel comfortable using a full range of financial services are not elementary forms of economic life shared across cultures or across political systems. The taken-for-granted notions about money management, savings, consumption, and investment are therefore amenable to sociological analysis.

Consider the spread of credit cards into the former Soviet Union. Alya Guseva (2008) examines the rise of the credit card market in Russia between 1998 and 2005 with a particular focus on how people use networks and on how institutions are created that enable merchants to trust that they would be paid. Institutions and social ties also helped banking institutions confidently share information without an overwhelming fear that the information would be misused. Her analysis could have engaged her subjects ethnographically with the intention of assessing the economic dispositions of credit card users and non-users, following an analogous strategy as that of Bourdieu in his study of Algerian workers during and after colonization.

If the economic instincts of individuals are taken to be variable, marketers, banks and nonprofit agencies can more effectively develop financial tools that fit the intuitions of specific populations. Rather than teach people that their economic instincts are wrong and have to radically change, some nonprofit agencies are trying to understand and take advantage of existing economic dispositions to promote economic goals of saving and investment; for example, asset building agencies such as the Mission Asset Fund (*Fondo Popular de la Misión*) in San Francisco utilizes *cestas* (baskets) – lending circles with a Latino twist – to promote asset building (Slambrouck 2010). José Quiñones, the executive director of the Mission Asset Fund, avers that the meanings and practices that already exist in the communities can be used to promote savings and investment practices so that the people meant to benefit from these programs do not feel that they are being asked to engage in practices that deny the worth of their beliefs, forcing them to go against their own sense of common sense.

As people make sense of their economic lives, they are often upholding, strengthening, or demolishing symbolic boundaries. Symbolic boundaries are the distinctions made between the attributes of objects, actions, or persons (Lamont and Fournier 1992). People engage in boundary work as they erect conceptual barriers between one category and another, and these categories tend to be hierarchical rather than merely categorical. In other words, the moral worth of one category becomes enhanced (or at least more visible) by virtue of its difference from another category. Symbolic boundaries help us see how price valuations (Velthuis 2005), moral distinctions (Lamont and Molnár 2001), and a sense of justifiable material inequalities are maintained. (Also see Wherry's discussion in Chapter 3 on how people are characterized by virtue of how they evaluate the prices of goods and services.)

One way that market boundaries are maintained is through ritual. A ritual is a series of acts performed for a sacred or solemn ceremony. They are "social occasions noted primarily for their symbolic, rather than utilitarian, purposes. They are a way of affirming the beliefs of the group and ... of attesting the continuity of the group's way of life and ideological commitment" (Biggart 1989: 153). Rituals constitute and represent markets. Take, for example, the social occasions in a large firm highlighting the charisma of its founders and sharing stories about how its leaders have overcome nearly insurmountable obstacles and have become stronger after experiencing harrowing journeys that tested the limits of their personal relationships, their organizational acumen, and the company's financial capacities. The firms (both large bureaucratic organizations and direct selling organizations such as Amway and Mary Kay) mount seminars, workshops, rallies, retreats, and other gatherings whose utilitarian goal of sharing information could be more cheaply organized.

By focusing on narratives, rituals, and face-to-face encounters, cultural sociologists can examine consequential processes that might have remained concealed in the error term of a regression equation. What are the rituals that buyers and sellers engage in? How tightly scripted are they? What are the scripts for these rituals? And what contributes to or precludes successful rituals that generate economic success versus failure? These questions are rather different from the usual emphasis on buyers and sellers focused on prices and the qualities of objects rather than on the meanings and emotions generated in a linked set of ritual interactions.

The field of inquiry is opening wide again, just as it did after Mark Granovetter's (1985) seminal statement on embeddedness, where he showed the consequences of social networks and societal institutions on markets. Rather than networks, this book looks to meaningful interactions; instead of institutions, this book places greater emphasis on collective narratives and cultural codes. Now it is time to clarify some of the core assumptions thus far hazily foretold.

Core Assumptions

A cultural sociology of markets differs from standard economic perspectives on how an economic actor is characterized, what the goals of economic action are, what strategies flow from those goals, and what are the nature of the markets in which these actions take place (Spillman 1999; 2011). Standard economic approaches focus on rational actors (model of economic actor) who derive utility from acquiring specific goods and services. This actor attempts to increase the combinations of goods and services that bring her the most satisfaction (primary goal), given her budget constraint. Her strategy is to realize her goal by employing cost-effective means. She acts alone, and as others who are acting alone in the marketplace to maximize their satisfaction bid on the same good or service, they encounter sellers who are trying to provide that good or service while both meeting their own costs of production and adding an extra charge so that they can generate a profit. Market prices result from the intersection of these two groups demanding and supplying goods or services in the marketplace.

A cultural perspective on market issues recognizes that the economic actor is pragmatic, but she also acts when her emotions peak; moreover, when affect does not spur her to action, her ingrained habits or societal rituals do. Her goals are multiple, combining material with ideational resources. Depending on the cultural understandings she shares with others, some goals are out of the question, while others are common sense. She does not always realize that she is trying to achieve a multitude of goals, and sometimes she disavows economic profits as her goal, yet economic profits remain one of her unspoken goals (and become more likely to be achieved as a result of her disavowal).

The strategies that she employs to meet her goals have meanings for her. They are not simply a way to change her state from A to B, a transition that may be accomplished in a variety of ways (technical feasibility) but that should be accomplished in a way that makes sense to her (cultural fit). Often the temporal ordering of action is also meaningful, with each step signifying something that makes the next step sensible and possible. The market she participates in (and creates in the act of participation) is sometimes a dramaturgical stage where she is taking on a role, offering a performance, interacting with an audience. At other times, it is a field with economic capital, cultural capital, and social capital arrayed as the poles of a force field, magnetically pulling her to appreciate some things but not others (tastes/preferences/ demand) or to associate with people who have similar accumulations of economic, cultural, and social capital (see Table 1).

130

Table 1. Economic and Cultural Depictions of Market Issues.

Market Issue	Markets as Economic Intentions	Markets as Cultural Intentions
Model of economic actor	Rational, utility function (with possibility of modeling emotion and habit)	Pragmatic, emotional, habitual (rational, utility function as one of many cultural orientations)
Goals of economic action	Optimization problem (allocation efficiency, maximize profits, minimize costs)	Multiple goals; some goals material, others symbolic; disavowal of some goals so that others realized; some potentially profitable moves "out of the question"; optimization problem as a cultural intention
Strategy of action	Means–end, purposive, instrumental rationality	Substantive, temporally (meaningfully) ordered, meaningfully instrumental
View of Market	Buyers–sellers; Supply–demand nexus	Fields, social performances, dramaturgically managed impressions, boundary work

Source: Adapted from Lyn Spillman, "Culture and Economic Life" (2011).

Strong and Weak Programs

One should understand the core assumptions cultural sociologists make about markets within the context of what Jeffrey Alexander and Philip Smith (Alexander 2003) call strong and weak programs. A strong program in culture recognizes culture as autonomous and often brackets out political and social structures along with non-symbolic resources in order to make the cultural texts operating in society appear with greater clarity. So long as the analyst regards culture as an autonomous force, the study can be said to be part of or approaching the strong program. If the analyst also specifies how culture and social texts manifest themselves in specific actors, actions, institutions and social situations, the study's qualifications for the strong program are assured.

The production of culture perspective exemplified by Richard Peterson and N. Anand exemplifies what Alexander and Smith (2003) call a weak program for cultural sociology. Peterson and Anand (2004) describe the six-facet model of cultural production. This model examines laws and regulations, technology, organizational structure, industry structure, occupational careers that facilitate or impede ongoing production, and the target groups for a product or service (market). Alexander and Smith argue that symbols and meaning influence the emergence of new cultural forms and that the six-facet model cannot explain why some products strike a resonant chord with some groups of people at particular periods of time but not with other groups and not during all time-periods.

These strong and weak cultural programs also have to be understood within Viviana Zelizer's (2010) discussion of extension, context, and alternative models of markets in economic sociology. Zelizer notes that some economic sociologists either extend rational choice models of behavior from economics to study a wide range of economic and social phenomena or they acknowledge that the contexts in which economic action is carried out affects how rational (profit maximizing) those actions will be. She contrasts these models with alternatives that use uniquely sociological concepts to describe and to explain markets and economic action. In this way, sociologists treat markets like any other branch of social life, such as religion, family, neighborhoods, and deviance. Zelizer exhorts

Table 2. Culture and Economic Outcomes in Strong Versus Weak Cultural Programs

Culture as Predictor of Economic Outcomes

		Yes	No
Markets Considered to be Cultural Intentions	**Yes**	Culture as structure, previously existing and multidimensional Economic action studied as ritual or social performance, meaningfully accomplished social action (Strong Program)	Culture as superstructure, resulting from social structure and material conditions Economic action as optimization problem only Tastes, preferences as outcomes of material conditions (Weak Program)
	No	Culture as structure, previously existing, and uni-dimensional (dummy variable) Economic action studied as a optimization problem with contextual constraints (Weak Program)	Culture as superstructure Tastes, preferences, understandings as properties of individuals and as idiosyncratic (Weak Program)

sociologists to use concepts developed within the field to examine markets as social and cultural phenomena.

Table 2 brings together how markets are studied when culture is treated as an autonomous force (the strong program in culture) and when sociologists use concepts unique to its discipline (alternative approach). Sociologists can also treat culture as a predictor of economic outcomes but can do so without treating culture as autonomous with its own structure and as imposing its own logics on market actors (weak program). These same sociologists may also opt for contextual analyses of how social conditions and cultural understandings (indicated by dummy variables) lead to various market outcomes.

When culture is not treated as a predictor of economic outcomes, it is the outcome of material conditions. Sociologists relying on Karl Marx (Marx [1859] 1978) or on Pierre Bourdieu (1984; 2005) can offer alternative explanations of how individuals and organizations generate surplus value in the cultural industries and how economically powerful actors capture the lion's share of the surplus value. Other sociologists and economists simply take culture to mean the idiosyncratic tastes and preferences of individuals and relegate culture to a realm that does not require explanation. There is no need to offer concepts unique to the field of sociology. Different cultures have different tastes, and the job of the analyst is to specify that there are different clusters of people who have different tastes.

Conclusion

Is a cultural sociology of markets really new? And how does one advance such a project? The cultural sociology of markets draws from cultural and economic sociologists and tries to show how a meaning-centered analysis (that sometimes brackets material and structural concerns) helps us see otherwise ignored mechanisms in the marketplace. By drawing on things people have already said (but have said in different disciplines or from different corners of the same discipline), there is a temptation to say that there is nothing new here, or that what is new simply can't be true. Robert K. Merton described this as the fallacy of adumbration. Alejandro Portes puts the fallacy like this: "[It] consists in negating the novelty of a scientific discovery by pointing to [its] earlier instances. In Merton's words ... the adumbrator believes that if something is new, it is not really true, and if something is true, it is not actually new. Precedents can always be found ... Yet, until the concept ... [is] coined and refined, the common character and significance of these phenomena remain obscure" (Portes 2001: 184). *The Culture of Markets* should help scholars connect dots that would have otherwise remained scattered. And if these dots are brought into focus, the field will move toward a more comprehensive understanding of how markets work.

References

Abolafia, Mitchell Y. 1996. *Making Markets: Opportunism and Restraint on Wall Street*. Cambridge, MA: Harvard University Press.

Akerlof, George A. and Rachel E. Kranton. 2010. *Identity Economics: How Our Identities Shape Our Work, Wages, and Well-Being*. Princeton: Princeton University Press.

Alden, William. 2011. "At Fed Chairman Bernanke's Press Conference, Stakes Are High." *Huffington Post*, April 27, 2011. http://www.huffingtonpost.com/2011/04/27/federal-reserve-bernanke-press_n_854126.html, accessed April 27, 2011.

Alexander, Jeffrey C. 2003. *The Meanings of Social Life: A Cultural Sociology*. New York: Oxford University Press.

Alexander, Jeffrey C. and Philip Smith. 2003. "The Strong Program in Cultural Sociology." pp. 11–26 in Alexander 2003.

Anderson, Elijah. 1999. "The Social Situation of the Black Executive: Black and White Identities in the Corporate World." pp. 3–29 in *The Cultural Territories of Race: Black and White Boundaries*, ed. M. Lamont. Chicago: University of Chicago Press.

Appadurai, Arjun. 1986. "Introduction: Commodities and the Politics of Value." pp. 3–63 in *The Social Life of Things: Commodities in Cultural Perspective*, ed. A. Appadurai. Cambridge: Cambridge University Press.

Arthur, W. Brian. 1989. "Competing Technologies, Increasing Returns, and Lock-In by Historical Events." *Economic Journal* 99: 116–31.

Bandelj, N. 2002. "Embedded Economies: Social Relations as Determinants of Foreign Direct Investment in Central and Eastern Europe." *SOCIAL FORCES* 81: 411–44.

Bandelj, Nina. 2003. "Particularizing the Global: Reception of Foreign Direct Investment in Slovenia." *Current Sociology* 51: 377–94.

References

—2008. *From Communists to Foreign Capitalists: The Social Foundations of Foreign Direct Investment in Postsocialist Europe*. Princeton: Princeton University Press.

Bandelj, Nina and Frederick F. Wherry. 2011. *The Cultural Wealth of Nations*. Palo Alto: Stanford University Press.

Barley, Stephen R. and Gideon Kunda. 1992. "Design and Devotion: Surges of Rational and Normative Ideolgoies of Control in Managerial Discourse." *Administrative Science Quarterly* 37: 363–99.

Becker, Howard S. 1953. "Becoming a Marihuana User." *American Journal of Sociology* 59: 235–42.

Berman, Laura. 2011. "The Chrysler Miracle." *Newsweek*, June 5, 2011. http://www.newsweek.com/2011/06/05/the-chrysler-miracle.html, accessed June 8, 2011.

Bernays, Edward L. 1928. "Manipulating Public Opinion: The Why and The How." *American Journal of Sociology* 33: 958–71.

Biggart, Nicole W and Mark Orrú. 1997. "Societal Strategic Advantage: Institutional Structure and Path Dependence in the Automotive and Electronics Industries of East Asia." pp. 201–39 in *State, Market, and Organizational Form*, ed. A. Bugra and B. Usdiken. Berlin: Walter de Gruyter.

Biggart, Nicole Woolsey. 1989. *Charismatic Capitalism: Direct Selling Organizations in America*. Chicago: University of Chicago Press.

Biggart, Nicole Woolsey and Mauro F. Guillén. 1999. "Developing Difference: Social Organization and the Rise of the Auto Industries of South Korea, Taiwan, Spain, and Argentina." *American Sociological Review* 64: 722–47.

Bourdieu, Pierre. 1984. *Distinction: A Social Critique of the Judgement of Taste*. Cambridge, MA: Harvard University Press.

—2000. "Making the Economic Habitus: Algerian Workers Revisited." *Ethnography* 1(1): 17–41.

—2005. *The Social Structures of the Economy*. Malden, MA: Polity.

Braudel, Fernand. 1981. *Civilization and Capitalism, 15th to 18th Century*, trans. S. Reynolds. New York: Harper and Row.

Burawoy, Michael. 1998. "The Extended Case Method." *Sociological Theory* 16(1): 4–33.

Carrington, Christopher. 1999. *No Place Like Home*. Chicago: University of Chicago Press.

Carruthers, Bruce G. and Sarah Babb. 1996. "The Color of Money and the Nature of Value: Greenbacks and Gold in Postbellum America." *American Journal of Sociology* 101: 1556–91.

Casino, Vincent J. Del and Stephen P. Hanna. 2000. "Representations and

References

Identities in Tourism Map Spaces." *Progress in Human Geography* 24: 23–46.

Certeau, Michel de. 1984. *The Practice of Everyday Life*. Berkeley: University of California Press.

Chin, Elizabeth. 2001. *Purchasing Power: Blacks, Kids and American Consumer Culture*. Minneapolis: University of Minnesota Press.

Christakis, Nicholas A. and James H. Fowler. 2007. "The Spread of Obesity in a Large Social Network Over 32 Years." *New England Journal of Medicine* 357: 370–9.

— 2008. "The Collective Dynamics of Smoking in a Large Social Network." *New England Journal of Medicine* 358: 2249–58.

Collins, Randall. 2004. *Interaction Ritual Chains*. Princeton, NJ: Princeton University Press.

Cook, Daniel Thomas. 2004. *The Commodification of Childhood: The Children's Clothing Industry and the Rise of the Child Consumer*. Durham: Duke University Press.

David, Paul A. 1986. "Understanding the Economics of QWERTY: The Necessity of History." pp. 30–49 in *Economic History and the Modern Economist*, ed. W. N. Parker. Oxford: Basil Blackwell.

DiMaggio, Paul. 1990. "Cultural Aspects of Economic Action and Organization." pp. 113–36 in *Beyond the Marketplace: Rethinking Economy and Society*, ed. R. Friedland and A. F. Robertson. New York: Aldine de Gruyter.

DiMaggio, Paul and Hugh Louch. 1998. "Socially Embedded Consumer Transactions: For What Kind of Purchases Do People Most Often Use Networks?" *American Sociological Review* 63: 619–37.

Dobbin, Frank. 1994. *Forging Industrial Policy: The United States, Britain, and France in the Railway Age*. New York: Cambridge University Press.

Dodd, Nigel. 1994. *The Sociology of Money*. Cambridge, MA: Polity.

Douglas, Mary and Baron Isherwood. 1979. *The World of Goods*. New York: Norton.

Durkheim, Emile. [1893] 1984. *The Division of Labor in Society*, trans. W. D. Halls. New York: Free Press.

—[1912] 1995. *The Elementary Forms of Religious Life*, trans. Karen E. Fields. New York: Simon and Schuster.

—[1957] 2005. *Professional Ethics and Civic Morals*, trans. Cornelia Brookfield. New York: Routledge.

Fishman, Robert M. 2006. "Introduction." pp. 1–14 in *The Year of the Euro: The Cultural, Social, and Political Import of Europe's Common Currency*, ed. R. M. Fishman and A. M. Messina. Notre Dame, IN: University of Notre Dame Press.

References

Fourcade, Marion and Kieran Healy. 2007. "Moral Views of Market Society." *Annual Review of Sociology* 33: 385–11.

Frankfort-Nachmias, Chava and David Nachmias. 2000. *Research Methods in the Social Sciences*. 6th edn. New York: Worth Publishers.

Friedland, Roger and A. F. Robertson. 1990. "Beyond the Marketplace." pp. 3–49 in *Beyond the Marketplace: Rethinking Economy and Society*, ed. R. Friedland and A. F. Robertson. New York: Aldine de Gruyter.

Geertz, Clifford. [1973] 2000. *The Interpretation of Cultures*. New York: Basic Books.

Gilbert, Emily and Eric Helleiner. 1999. "Introduction–Nation-states and Money: Historical Contexts, Interdisciplinary Perspectives." pp. 1–20 in *Nation-States and Money: The Past, Present and Future of National Currencies*, ed. E. Gilbert and E. Helleiner. New York: Routledge.

Goffman, Erving. 1967. *Interaction Ritual*. New York: Vintage.

Granovetter, Mark. 1985. "Economic Action and Social Structure: The Problem of Embeddedness." *American Journal of Sociology* 91: 481–510.

—1995. "The Economic Sociology of Firms and Entrepreneurs." pp. 128–65 in *The Economic Sociology of Immigration: Essays on Networks, Ethnicity, and Entrepreneurship*, ed. A. Portes. New York: Russell Sage Foundation.

Griswold, Wendy. 1981. "American Character and the American Novel." *American Journal of Sociology* 86: 740–65.

Guseva, Alya. 2008. *Into the Red: The Birth of the Credit Card Market in Postcommunist Russia*. Palo Alto: Stanford University Press.

Harvey, David. 2010. *The Enigma of Capital: And the Crises of Capitalism*. New York: Oxford University Press.

Haveman, Heather A. and Hayagreeva Rao. 2006. "Hybrid Forms and the Evolution of Thrifts." *American Behavioral Scientist* 49: 974–986.

Healy, Kieran. 2000. "Embedded Altruism: Blood Collection Regimes and the European Union's Donor Population." *American Journal of Sociology* 105: 1633–57.

—2006. *Last Best Gifts: Altruism and the Market for Human Blood and Organs*. Chicago: University of Chicago Press.

Helleiner, Eric. 1998. "National Currencies and National Identities." *American Behavioral Scientist* 41: 1409–36.

Ho, Karen. 2009. *Liquidated: An Ethnography of Wall Street*. Durham, NC: Duke University Press.

Holt, Douglas B. 2004. *How Brands Become Icons: The Principles of Cultural Branding*. Boston: Harvard Business School Press.

Hymans, Jacques E.C. 2004. "The Changing Color of Money: European Currency Iconography and Collective Identity." *European Journal of International Relations* 10: 5–31.

References

—2006. "Money for Mars? The Euro Banknotes and European Identity." pp. 15–36 in *The Year of the Euro: The Cultural, Social, and Political Import of Europe's Common Currency*, ed. R. M. Fishman and A. M. Messina. Notre Dame, IN: University of Notre Dame Press.

Jackall, Robert. [1988] 2010. *Moral Mazes: The World of Corporate Managers*. New York: Oxford University Press.

King, Gary, Robert O. Keohane, and Sidney Verba. 1994. *Designing Social Inquiry: Scientific Inference in Qualitative Research*. Princeton: Princeton University Press.

Knorr-Cetina, Karin. 2009. "The Synthetic Situation: Interactionism for a Global World." *Symbolic Interaction* 32: 61–87.

Knorr-Cetina, Karin and Urs Bruegger. 2002. "Global Microstructures: The Virtual Societies of Financial Markets." *American Journal of Sociology* 107: 905–50.

Kopytoff, Igor. 1986. "The Cultural Biography of Things: Commoditization as Process." pp. 64–94 in *The Social Life of Things: Commodities in Cultural Perspective*, ed. A. Appadurai. Cambridge: Cambridge University Press.

Krauss, Clifford. 2001. "To Weather Recession, Argentines Revert to Barter." In *The New York Times*. May 6, 2001.

Lamont, Michèle and Marcel Fournier. 1992. *Cultivating Differences: Symbolic Boundaries and the Making of Inequality*. Chicago: The University of Chicago Press.

Lamont, Michèle and Virág Molnár. 2001. "How Blacks Use Consumption to Shape Their Collective Identity: Evidence from Marketing Specialists." *Journal of Consumer Culture* 1: 31–45.

Lang, Peter. 1994. *LETS Work: Rebuilding the Local Economy*. Bristol, UK: Gover Books.

Leach, William. 1984. "Transformations in a Culture of Consumption: Women and Department Stores, 1890–1925." *Journal of American History* 71: 319–42.

Lee, Ching Kwan. 1998. *Gender and the South China Miracle: Two Worlds of Factory Women*. Berkeley: University of California Press.

Levin, Peter. 2001. "Gendering the Market: Temporality, Work, and Gender on a National Futures Exchange." *Work and Occupations* 28: 112–30.

Lietaer, Bernard A. 2001. *The Future of Money: A New Way to Create Wealth, Work and a Wiser World*. London: Century.

Light, Ivan H. and Steven J. Gold. 2000. *Ethnic Economies*. San Diego, CA: Academic.

Light, Ivan H. and Stavros Karageorgis. 1994. "The Ethnic Economy." In *The Handbook of Economic Sociology*, ed. N. J. Smelser and R. Swedberg.

References

New York and Princeton: The Russell Sage Foundation and Princeton University Press.

Lizardo, Omar. 2006. "How Cultural Tastes Shape Personal Networks." *American Sociological Review* 71: 778–807.

Marx, Karl. [1859] 1978. "Preface to *A Contribution to the Critique of Political Economy.*" pp. 3–6 in *The Marx–Engels Reader*, ed. R. C. Tucker. New York: W.W. Norton Company.

Marx, Karl and Friedrich Engels. [1835] 2004. *The German Ideology.* New York: International Publishers.

Merton, Robert. 1957. *Social Theory and Social Structure.* Glencoe, IL: Free Press.

Mooney, Margarita. 2003. "Migrants Social Ties in the U.S. and Investment in Mexico." *Social Forces* 49: 1455–70.

Morrill, Calvin. 1995. *The Executive Way: Conflict Management in Corporations.* Chicago: University of Chicago Press.

Muniz, Jr., Albert M. and Thomas C. O'Guinn. 2001. "Brand Community." *Journal of Consumer Research* 27: 412–32.

Nuttavuthisit, Krittinee. 2007. "Branding Thailand: Correcting the Negative Image of Sex Tourism." *Place Branding and Public Diplomacy* 3: 21–30.

Nye, John V. C. 2007. *War, Wine, and Taxes: The Political Economy of Anglo-French Trade, 1689–1900.* Princeton, NJ: Princeton University Press.

Peterson, Richard A. and N. Anand. 2004. "The Production of Culture." *Annual Review of Sociology* 30: 311–34.

Podolny, Joel. 2005. *Status Signals.* Princeton, NJ: Princeton University Press.

Polanyi, Karl. [1944] 1957. *The Great Transformation.* Boston: Beacon.

Portes, Alejandro. 2001. "Introduction: The Debates and Significance of Immigrant Transnationalism." *Global Networks* 1: 181–94.

Portes, Alejandro and Alex Stepick. 1994. *City on the Edge: The Transformation of Miami.* Berkeley: University of California Press.

Preda, Alex. 2008. "Brief Encounters: Calculation and the Interaction Order of Anonymous Electronic Markets." *Accounting, Organizations and Society* 34: 675–93.

Ritzer, George. 1999. *Enchanting a Disenchanted World: Revolutionizing the Means of Consumption.* Thousand Oaks, CA: Pine Forge Press.

Rivera, Lauren. 2008. "Managing 'Spoiled' National Identity: War, Tourism and Memory in Croatia." *American Sociological Review* 73: 613–34.

—2011. "Ivies, Extracurriculars, and Exclusion: Elite Employers' Use of Educational Credentials." *Research in Social Stratification and Mobility* 29: 71–90.

References

Rohter, Larry. 2001. "Argentina's Stopgap Cash Gets Some Funny Looks." In *The New York Times*. August 21, 2001.

Royster, Deirdre A. 2003. *Race and the Invisible Hand: How White Networks Exclude Black Men from Blue-Collar Jobs*. Berkeley: University of California Press.

Sahlins, Marshall. 1976. *Culture and Practical Reason*. Chicago: University of Chicago Press.

Schor, Juliet. 2004. *Born to Buy: The Commercialized Child and the New Consumer Culture*. New York: Schribner.

Schudson, Michael. 1984. *Advertising, the Uneasy Persuasion: Its Dubious Impact on American Society*. New York: Basic Books.

Shalev, Michael. 2009. "'Loyalty Benefits' and the Welfare State." In *The Social Contract Revisited*: The Foundation for Law, Justice and Society in collaboration with The Centre for Socio-Legal Studies, University of Oxford, www.fljs.org.

Slambrouck, Paul van. 2010. "My Lender, My Friend: Lending Circles with a Latino Twist." In *Christian Science Monitor*.

Small, Mario Luis. 2009. " 'How Many Cases Do I Need?' On Science and the Logic of Case Selection in Field-based Research." *Ethnography* 10: 5–38.

Smelser, Neil and Richard Swedberg. 1994. *The Handbook of Economic Sociology*. Princeton: Princeton University Press.

Smith, Charles W. 1989. *Auctions: The Social Construction of Value*. New York Free Press.

Somers, Margaret R. and Fred Block. 2005. "From Poverty to Perversity: Ideas, Markets and Institutions over 200 Years of Welfare Debate." *American Sociological Review* 70: 260–87.

Spillman, Lyn. 1999. "Enriching Exchange: Cultural Dimensions of Markets." *American Journal of Economics and Sociology* 58: 1047–71.

—2011. "Culture and Economic Life." In *The Oxford Handbook of Cultural Sociology*, ed. J. Alexander, P. Smith, and R. Jacobs. New York: Oxford University Press.

Stark, David. 2009. *The Sense of Dissonance*. Princeton: Princeton University Press.

Steinmetz, George. 2004. "Odious Comparisons: Incommensurability, the Case Study, and 'Small N's' in Sociology." *Sociological Theory* 22, 3: 371–400.

Sutton, Francis X., Seymour E. Harris, Carl Kaysen, and James Tobin. 1956. *The American Business Creed*. Cambridge, MA: Harvard University Press.

Thaler, Richard H. 1999. "Mental Accounting Matters." *Journal of Behavioral Decision Making* 12: 183–206.

References

Thornton, Patricia H. and William Ocasio. 1999. "Institutional Logics and the Historical Contingency of Power in Organizations: Executive Succession in the Higher Education Publishing Industry, 1958–1990." *American Journal of Sociology* 105: 801–44.

Tversky, Amos and Daniel Kahneman. 1981. "The Framing Decisions and the Rationality of Choice." *Science* 211: 453–8.

Tye, Larry. 1998. *The Father of Spin: Edward L. Bernays and the Birth of Public Relations.* New York: Crown.

Vaughan, Diane. 1996. *The Challenger Launch Decision: Risky Technology, Culture, and Deviance at NASA.* Chicago: University of Chicago Press.

Velthuis, Olav. 2003. "Symbolic Meanings of Prices: Constructing the Value of Contemporary Art in Amsterdam and New York Galleries." *Theory and Society* 32: 181–215.

—2005. *Talking Prices: Symbolic Meanings of Prices on the Market for Contemporary Art.* Princeton: Princeton University Press.

Weber, Klaus, Kathryn L. Heinze, and Michaela DeSouzey. 2008. "Forage for Thought: Mobilizing Codes in the Movement for Grass-fed Meat and Dairy Products." *Adminitrative Science Quarterly* 53: 529–67.

Weber, Max. [1922] 1978. *Economy and Society: An Outline of Interpretive Sociology.* Berkeley and Los Angeles: University of California Press.

—[1905] 2008. *The Protestant Ethic and the Spirit of Capitalism with Other Writings on the Rise of the West*, trans. Stephen Kalberg. New York: Oxford University Press.

Wherry, Frederick F. 2007. "Trading Impressions: Evidence from Costa Rica." *The Annals of the American Academy of Political and Social Science* 610: 217–31.

—2008. *Global Markets and Local Crafts: Thailand and Costa Rica Compared.* Baltimore: Johns Hopkins University Press.

—forthcoming) "Performance Circuits in the Marketplace." *Politics and Society.*

Whitford, Josh. 2005. *The New Old Economy: Networks, Institutions, and the Organizational Transformation of American Manufacturing.* New York: Oxford University Press.

—2012. "Waltzing, Relational Work and the Construction (or not) of Collaboration in Manufacturing Industries." *Politics and Society.*

Williamson, Oliver E. 1981. "The Economics of Organization: The Transaction Cost Approach." *American Journal of Sociology* 87: 548–77.

Wuthnow, Robert. 1996. *Poor Richard's Principles: Recovering the American Dream through the Moral Dimension of Work, Business, and Money.* Princeton: Princeton University Press.

References

Zaloom, Caitlin. 2006. *Out of the Pits: Traders and Technology from Chicago to London*. Chicago: University of Chicago Press.

Zelizer, Viviana A. 1989. "The Social Meaning of Money: 'Special Monies'." *American Journal of Sociology* 95: 342–77.

—2001. "Sociology of Money." pp. 991–4 in *International Encyclopedia of Social and Behavioral Sciences*, vol. 15, ed. N. J. Smelser and P. B. Baltes. Amsterdam: Elsevier.

—2005. *The Purchase of Intimacy*. Princeton: Princeton University Press.

—2010. *Economic Lives: How Culture Shapes the Economy*. Princeton: Princeton University Press.

Zuckerman, Ezra W. 1999. "The Categorical Imperative: Securities Analysts and the Illegitimacy Discount." *American Journal of Sociology* 104: 1398–438.

Zuckerman, Ezra W., Tai-Young Kim, Kalinda Ukanwa, and James von Rittmann. 2003. "Robust Identities or Nonentities? Typecasting in the Feature-Film Labor Market." *American Journal of Sociology* 108: 1018–74.

Zukin, Sharon. 2004. *Point of Purchase: How Shopping Changed American Culture*. New York: Routledge.

Index

Index

146

Index

Index

Index

Index

Index

Index

Index

Index

155

Index

Index